SOLDIER POETRY

of the

SECOND WORLD WAR

AN ANTHOLOGY

Selected and Arranged by
JANE & WALTER MORGAN

Presented with the permission of the
DEPARTMENT OF NATIONAL DEFENCE
Government of Canada

MOSAIC PRESS
Oakville-New York-London

CANADIAN CATALOGUING IN PUBLICATION DATA

Soldier poetry of the Second World War

ISBN 0-88962-473-9 (bound) ISBN 0-88962-472-0 (pbk.)
1. World War, 1939-1945 - Poetry. 2. Canadian poetry (English) - 20th century.*
3. War poetry, Canadian (English).* 4. Soldiers' writings, Canadian.
I. Morgan, Jane, 1913-   . II. Morgan, Walter, 1911-   .

PS8287.W37S64 1990   C811'.5208'0358   C90-095632-1   PR9195.85.W37S64 1990

Published by MOSAIC PRESS, P.O. Box 1032, Oakville, Ontario, L6J 5E9, Canada. Offices and warehouse at 1252 Speers Road, Units #1&2, Oakville, Ontario, L6L 5N9, Canada.

Mosaic Press acknowledges the assistance of the Canadian Council and the Ontario Arts Council in support of its publishing programme.

Copyright ©Jane & Walter Morgan, 1990
Design by Marion Black
Typeset by Jackie Ernst
Printed and bound in Canada.

ISBN 0-88962-470-2 PAPER   ISBN 0-88962-473-9 CLOTH

MOSAIC PRESS:
in Canada:
        MOSAIC PRESS, 1252 Speers Road, Units # 1&2, Oakville, Ontario, L6L 5N9, P.O. Box 1032, Oakville, Ontario, L6J 5E9, Canada.

In the United States:
        Distributed to the trade in the United States by: National Book Network, Inc., 4720-A Boston Way, Lanham, MD 20706, USA.

In the U.K. and Europe by:
        SPA Books Ltd., P.O. Box 47, Stevenage, Herts, SG2 8UH, U.K.

Table of Contents

Acknowledgements

We would like to express our gratitude for the support and assistance we received from the Department of National Defence, the Department of Veterans' Affairs, the Public Archives, Ottawa, the C.B.C. and the *Legion Magazine*. We are grateful for the services offered us by the librarians in the Cookstown, Barrie and Metro Toronto libraries. We are deeply indebted to J. Douglas MacFarlane and George Powell for the encouragement and advice they have given us during the assembling of these poems. Lastly, we would like to thank the members of our family for their interest in our project, especially David, whose painstaking work brought the manuscript to a satisfactory conclusion.

Walter and Jane Morgan
September, 1990

About the Editors

Walter C. Morgan was born into a family of four boys and one daughter, and two older half brothers, where there were always discussions about soldiering and armory. The two half-brothers served in The First World War and three of the brothers in the Second World War.

Walter volunteered for service overseas with Canadian R.G.E.M.E. in April 1940. In 1942, he married F. Jane Morgan and has three daughters. Landing in France shortly after D Day, Walter saw service in France, Belgium, Holland and Germany, obtaining the rank of Armorer/Q.M.S. Upon returning to civilian life he attended United College in Winnipeg and subsequently obtained employment in the Post Office in a supervisory capacity. Since his retirement he has been associated with The Ontario Rifle Association.

Jane Morgan taught in Winnipeg Schools, at Balmoral Hall, and was Lecturer and Assistant Professor at The University of Manitoba. She obtained her Ph.D in French Letters from the University of Ottawa in 1977.

Walter and Jane Morgan are retired and reside in the Cookstown area, Ontario.

Editions Of The Maple Leaf

Italy:	Naples/Rome	January 1944 - March 1945
France:	Caen	July 1944 - September 1944
Belgium:	Brussels	September 1944 - September 1945

Western Europe

Holland:	Amsterdam	September 1945 - February 1946
Britain:	London	July 1945 - February 1946
Germany:	Delmenhorst	November 1945 - May 1946

All references at the end of each poem in this volume refer to *The Maple Leaf*.

Preface

It's a safe bet that most Second War servicemen and women didn't know an Iambic from a Pentameter but that didn't stop a surprising number of them writing poetry. This quickly became evident when the Canadian Army newspaper, *The Maple Leaf*, introduced a feature titled "Rhyme and Reason", a weekly collection of soldier poems.

Before long, the poetry became one of the most popular features of the paper, both from a reader's and contributor's standpoint. Maybe it's because there's a bit of poet in most human beings, just waiting a chance for expression.

In this collection, Walter and Jane Morgan have recorded impressive testimony to the poetic talents of the Canadian soldiers. From Naples to Rome, from Caen to Brussels to Amsterdam to Delmenhorst, editions of *The Maple Leaf* produced an amazing variety of material.

Great credit is due the Morgans for the idea in the first place, and for the painstaking research and organization involved in the book's production. I know this was a labour of love and I feel sure that you will love the labour.

J. Douglas MacFarlane
(Managing Editor of *The Maple Leaf*)

Introductory Note

This book presents the selected poems from *The Maple Leaf*. The anthology is arranged thematically but all the poems are referenced as to where they were written. The poems written in Italy where *The Maple Leaf* was first printed are a closely-knit group, and present no real difficulties. After D-Day and the heavy fighting which took place in Picardy and Normandy, a western edition was initiated and issued from Caen for a short time under difficult circumstances. In September of 1944 the editors from Caen and their staff moved to Brussels where there were better facilities. Here they were joined by the team from Italy. This assembly of experienced editors, reporters, writers, photographers, cartoonists, printers, and others had to cover a more widely spread area, but had much superior facilities. "Strange Harvest", describing the heavy fighting which took place in the vicinity of Caen, was published in Brussels, as were some poems written in Holland and Germany. Presses were later established in Amsterdam and Delmenhorst. Poems were sometimes published several months after they were composed; others were found on the bodies of fallen comrades and submitted by their friends.

The Maple Leaf was not issued in Britain until May of 1945 and contains little or no poetry. The creative energy unleashed by the experiences, dangers, and horrors of war was exhausted; men were above all anxious to be home. Some of the poems were probably composed earlier in England, the others in retrospect from other lands. Altogether they give a glimpse of England at war: the watch on the coast, and also inland by the Home Guard, the bombing raids, the resilience of the civil population, and the presence of the Canadian soldiers, many of whom married girls from the British Isles.

Indeed, each area of warfare seems to have its own peculiar flavour. While recounting the hardships and personal commitment demanded by war, the poems from Italy reflect something of the musical rhymes and ambience of the Mediterranean lands, and those from France the cruelty and excitement of mortal combat. The verses from Belgium reveal the shadows of Flanders Fields and a release of tensions. In those from Holland we read the grave thoughts of men confronted with the distress of a defeated and occupied nation, and with the necessity of future plans for peace and brotherhood.

Poets are not historians, although we read descriptions of the battles fought at Ortona, Cassino, Portecorvo, and Rimini in Italy, at the beachhead and Falaise Gap in France, at the Battle of the Scheldt in Holland. But these poets give us a more intimate account of these conflicts and together they project the rhythm of the war.

In general, the poetry of war has a well defined range of subject matter: the call-to-arms, statement of purpose, descriptions of battles fought, grief at the loss of a friend, or respect for the dead. The poems of the Maple Leaf go beyond these narrow confines. They make their own call-to-arms and repeat it frequently. The cause for which they are fighting is clearly expressed; by general consent it is for freedom and justice and for the protection of their own countrymen from the evils of war.

This theme takes on a religious note in the words of Padre Higgs:

> They do not ask a golden cease fire,
> Or a tower of graven stone,
> But that men may live in a world set free
> From guilt, by their blood atoned.

Living in the open air, except in the depths of winter, soldiers curse the mountains of Italy, its mud, and the water-logged terrain of Holland. But elsewhere they regard nature as "the fountain of all goodness", symbol of eternal life. They are compassionate when they view the ruined cities, and the distress of the bereaved, bewildered, hungry children. They share the joy of those they liberate, and accept their hospitality and friendship.

To fully appreciate these poems, the contemporary reader must consider them within the context of the 'forties', when Canada was a Dominion with stronger ties to Britain than to the U.S.A., who entered the War later on. It was an era when Christianity was a living force within the hearts and minds of men and women, and the preservation of Christian principles was of paramount importance. Today we speak in lay terms of "values", "ethics", "human rights", and the "peace process".

The purpose of *The Maple Leaf* was to supply the troops with news from home and abroad, and to freely express the thoughts and opinions of its readers. A poem could therefore express and reflect upon the ordeals and experiences of not only one man, its author, but of many men; we are speaking of People's Poetry. The poems contributed to the high morale maintained within the Canadian Army and all were sustained by their positive approach to warfare. The poets took their cue not from the realistic verses of Wilfred Owen and Siegfried Sassoon of the First World War, but rather from the idealism of Rupert Brooke and John McCrae. The image of the torch and our responsibilities to the Dead are taken up in many pages of this volume of poetry. In our contemporary anti-heroic society, writers of best-sellers and new biographies, as well as producers of films, find it both satisfying and lucrative to focus on the weaknesses of traditional heroes, heroines, and deities. But our poets of the 'forties accepted and respected the ideals of heroic action and personal sacrifice.

There are lighter moments, of course, with a sense of warmth and cheerfulness under adverse circumstances, supported by the cartoons, pin-ups, and comic-strips reproduced in *The Maple Leaf*. In periods of rest there is time to reflect, to philosophize, to make plans for the future, to dream, and to think nostalgically of Canada, wives, sweethearts, and loved ones.

Yet there is within these poems a realization of the evil present in the world. The Allies defeated the Nazi forces, but could not eradicate the evil they engendered, nor foresee the underground presence of the Nazis in other lands in later years. What is remarkable in the poems is the ever-present desire for peace and brotherhood. From these aspirations has emerged the strength of the Canadian Peace Corps, playing its part now in the troubled areas of the globe. Some poets speak prophetically, as in the following stanza:

Let men heed not to colour,
 Nor criticize of creed;
Abolish, Good Lord, from them
 Their greatest foe--greed.

  Soldier-poets have always existed, such as the Crusader-Troubadours, Sir Philip Sidney, Colonel Lovelace, Wilfred Owen, John McCrae, Earl Birney, Gary Geddes, and Douglas Le Pan. But in *The Maple Leaf* we are not speaking of the work of professional poets, but of the efforts of many men of various occupations and from varied backgrounds. This phenomenon has been well explained by Lt. Col. Gilchrist in his introduction to "Booklet of Poems" published in Rome, Italy, by the Canadian Public Relations Services in February, 1945.

  "Give a soldier a stub of pencil and a piece of paper and the first thing you know he's written a poem. Maybe all men are poets at heart and it just takes a war to awaken that hidden talent.... Perhaps it is because there is plenty of time to think in the army. Those long vigils when dug in and waiting for something to happen, those black, bleak nights when sleep will not come, give plenty of opportunity to think, to look inside oneself.... It is then very often, by the light of a guttering candle, in some shell-blasted casa or in some nice, cozy slit-trench, that poems are born."

  The poems contributed to the Rhyme and Reason columns of *The Maple Leaf* vary in quality from the familiar to the well-turned sonnet and skillfully crafted verses. They are mainly written in traditional form and rhetoric remembered from school days, although a few are in the freer verse form as used by Earl Birney in "This Page My Pigeon" (Portsmouth, 1944) and "The Road to Nijmegen" (Holland, 1945). Rhyme was still considered essential to poetry in the 'forties', and the general tenor of *The Maple Leaf* demanded Reason. Poets had to have something important to say. To quote from "Ogden Nashiism", generally speaking this collection is "according to the brow not high". This is the poetry of commitment, where content is sometimes more important than form. Nor are we yet in an era of narcissistic musings, extended trivia, or of verse which tease the mind through a series of interpretations. This is poetry generated by violence.

These poems have been lying dormant for many years, remembered only by the men who wrote them and those who read them. Some were mentioned by Leonard Brockington on a CBC Radio programme during the War. George W. Powell, poetry editor of *The Maple Leaf* in Italy, presented some of the more humorous poems in a Remembrance Day feature on CJOH, Ottawa, in 1987. ''The Maple Leaf Forever'' by Barry D. Rowland and J. D. MacFarlane published in 1987, which gives the history of the newspaper and details of its publication, together with facsimile pages from the original issue, caused a rebirth of interest in this wartime venture. We feel it is the appropriate moment to bring this collection of poems gleaned from the pages of *The Maple Leaf* to the attention of today's readers. We apologize for any omissions or inaccuracies which may have occurred during the assembly of these poems, and regret that it proved impossible to reach the poets or their families.

Walter and Jane Morgan
September, 1990

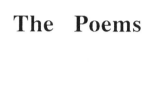

The   Poems

I

Heroism

Our Cape Breton Highlanders

These are our boys--
The boys who lived next door or down the street,
The boys who whistled on their way to school,
Or else, with laggard feet,
Stopped to toss pebbles in a wayside pool,
Knocked marbles 'gainst a fence or wall.
These are the boys
Whose names were written in registers a few short years ago;
Such wide-eyed boys, just five or six or so,
Who, now to manhood grown, have heard the call
And answered with their lives if need be,
So that other little boys of five or six or so
May still be free
To whistle on their way to school,
Or, with reluctant feet,
Stop to toss pebbles in a wayside pool,
Play marbles on the street.

Margaret Nickerson

Italy: Vol. I, No. 77, pg. 5   *May 6, 1944*

Canada - Our Home, Our Pride

Mighty as the oceans wide.
At the call to arms we came,
Pledged our help, in freedom's name.
Loving justice, scorning fear,
Ever with our purpose near.

Loving kinfolk, far away,
Eager for the happy day,
Armistice! Then let it be,
Final, glorious victory.

D. B. Holliday

Italy: Vol. 1, No. 83, pg. 5　　　*May 13, 1944*

Beyond St. Vito Road[4]

(Dedicated to Major Paul Triquet, V.C., and his men.)

If you travel to St. Vito
Turning northward by the sea,
You will hear the crescendo
Of our field artillery.
You will feel the earth a-trembling
With shell and bomb and mine,
You will know the Hun is short'ning
Once again, his Winter line.

Puffs of smoke will be arising
East to west along the line,
And our troops will be advancing
In the face of shell and mine.
This one sector must be wrested
In our world-wide battle plan;
For the issues here contested
Will decide the fate of Man.

You will carry with you memories,
When you leave that muddy line,
Stretching north through hills and gullies
Where the bullets hiss and whine;
Where above, our airplanes are dipping
To unloose their precious load.
While below, the men are praying--
Just beyond St. Vito Road.

You'll praise the gallant infantry
Who climbed the steep terrain
To storm Ortono by the sea
In mud, and frost and rain;
You'll say a prayer for all the youth .
That dwells in Death's abode,
Who gave their all for God and Truth
Beyond St. Vito Road.

J. M. Colling
Italy: Vol. I, No. 83, pg. 5   *May 13, 1944*

The Infantry

Where soldiers, wearied from the fray
Whose faith alone remains
To give them courage, so that they
Can hold secure their gains,
Who hold no fear for life nor health
Of nights on foreign sod,
And laugh aloud at death itself,
Their faith is in their God.

Muddy trenches, water filled,
In pill-box bleak and cold
They stand their watch though damp and chilled
While dramas of the night unfold.
Where shad'wy forms in starlit mist
When moving to and fro
Are halted, secret password hissed
And challenge answered, soft and low.

While tracer paints the darkened sky
With intricate designs,
Patrols go out and brave men die,
Far out behind the German lines.
Midst thump of shrapnel falling near
While mortars sob and moan
They do their job untouched by fear
Each man a hero on his own.

They dream sweet dreams of future times,
When war and strife shall cease
And poignant thoughts run through their minds
Of happy homes and peace.
They hold no terror of the foe
His power nor of his might.
They trust in God, for well they know
The cause for which they fight.

Alert and silent, brave and strong
They hold their lives at stake.
For well they know where they belong
They fight for freedom's sake.
They do their's with laugh and jest
While long hours pass away.
Till time when they lie down to rest- -
When dawn unveils another day.

M. St. C. Sterling

Italy: Vol. I, No. 95, pg. 5   *May 27, 1944*

Front-Line Johnnies

'Twas a sultry day of battle
Muddy Melfa flowed below
And all hell was appoppin'
'Bove the water's undertow.
When thru' the smoke-filled valley
Charged two men chock full of guts
Blasting for themselves an alley
Thru' the truck and trailer ruts.
Remember, Hell was breaking loose
Hot missiles screamed around
But our heroes, both undaunted
Streaked for ever higher ground.
It wasn't that they shunned the noise
Or yet the flying lead
They simply wished to occupy
A slit-trench straw-filled bed.
Diving o'er the parapet
They heard the Spandaus rattle
And Taylor said to Heahy
B Ech is in a battle.
We must advance to give them aid
If only as a favour
Besides I left with Georgie Pitt
My gum and last Life Saver.
The battle soon was over
As down the line they came
And they were really "toasted"
These undaunted guys gained fame.
And now they lounge at well-earned ease
Swilling beer and Vino
As they await their two V. C.'s
These heroes of Cassino.

Buster (N. B. H.)

Italy: Vol. II, No. 12, pg. 5   July 15, 1944

'Twas Not in Vain

Once more we have our "Flanders Field"--
Again the poppies grow,
And like the last great fight, we see
The crosses row on row;
For brave men lie 'neath foreign soil
In lasting peace and free from toil.

Who knows their thought as they passed on
To that Great Land above?
With dimming eyes I'm sure they saw
Their homes--the ones they loved;
They gave up life, the price supreme,
To rid the world of a madman's dream.

How gallantly they fought and died;
Their last wish was that we
Would carry on; they knew one day
They'd share our victory;
So we'll keep the faith and thus they'll know
They helped make peace on Earth below.

As in the last war, so in this,
God calls men to his side,
They'll live in joy eternal--
We'll think of them with pride;
And well we may, they gave up all
That good might live and evil fall.

So sleep, brave warriors, you must know
The years can never dim
Your mem'ry, valor, sacrifice,
As now you rest with Him.
We'll make a world where free folk reign,
And then you'll know--'twas not in vain.

George Downie

Italy: Vol. II, No. 18, pg. 5   *July 22, 1944*

The Silent Martyrs

Destruction and atrocities
Are kindred things of war,
That makes us wonder if this world
Is still worth fighting for.
A world where murdering monsters
Can stalk defenseless prey,
As were our nineteen comrades
Taken prisoners in the fray.

At the mercy of their captors,
They kept their lips tight sealed
And they, despite a threat of death,
No word of plan revealed.
How high they staked their honour
(God rest these gallant men)
Rang loud and clear around the earth,
From a hallowed Norman glen.

They were murdered by the Nazis--
The "Kultured" fiends of hell--
When they hear the bells of Victory
Sounding strong the German knell.
But Canadians will remember
When the battles have been won,
The death of nineteen silent martyrs--
And justice will be done.

May God, too, judge the killers
In trial by Bible truth,
And the guilty will be sentenced--
Eye for eye and tooth for tooth.

James Pearson

Italy: Vol. II, No. 42, pg. 5   *August 19, 1944*

In Memoriam

(this verse was written by the wife of a sergeant in the Ld. SH who was killed during Melfa River action.)

It seems he was too young to die
Yet, had he lived a normal span
Could he have left a finer record?
Would he have died a better man?

He has gone out to meet his Maker,
Full of the charity of Youth,
Serving his fellows boldly, bravely,
Fighting a battle for the Truth.

Many an old and hardened heart
Would envy him--his youthful fame,
His dear, brief life, his ardent soul,
His noble end, his honoured name.

Anonymous

Italy: Vol. II, No. 78, pg. 5   September 30, 1944

From the Royal Canadian Airforce
to the Active Canadian Army
(Volunteers All)

To all our pals in battledress
From us in air force blue,
Here's luck and best of hunting
To the last jack man of you!
The way things look to us right now,
It won't be very long
Before in person, you'll collect
For comrades of Hong Kong.
For every khaki-clad Canuck,
Who made the sacrifice,
The Prince of Darkness and his friends
Will pay a bitter price.
And Bertchesgarten's bogus seer
Will finally confess--
"I might have licked the world but for
These men in battledress!"

W/C Creed, R.C.A.F.

Italy: Vol. II, No. 84, pg. 5   *October 7, 1944*

The Home Guard

We all know now how Englishmen who day by day
Were shopkeepers, workingmen, who didn't earn much pay,
How clerks and others in black coats and collars white
Gave all the time they had to find out how to fight
Should an invader land. Night after night and weekends, too,
They worked and trained; all of them knew
They stood alone. They weren't dismayed, not they,
Those average men of Britain of whom the world can say
"You led the fight for Freedom."

G. A. Rose

Italy: Vol. II, No. 84, pg. 5   *October 7, 1944*

Strange Harvest

Dip gently your scythe good reaper,
O'er the fields of Calvados.
Tread softly Normandy's furrowed earth
From Epron to the coast.
For the harvest is not all the yield of the soil,
Nor the furrows the mark of the plough,
But earth's rich red is the blood of the dead,
The dead who are sleeping now.
They came from the sea, like you and me,
But they beached on a steel-rimmed coast.
They carved their way through the Hun at bay,
And blasted the tyrant's boast
That no might could breach the wave-locked shore,
No Allied foot gain hold:
The sea would be red with the blood of the dead,
The dead that had been too bold.

On their left and right were Britain's men,
And from south of the Forty-nine,
Came the western flanks of the Allied ranks
Through mortar, shell and mine.
The wall was stormed, the beaches won,
The skies grew sullen and wild,
Till the strength of the mighty men of the sea
Seemed less than the strength of a child.
Three precious weeks they fought each yard
From their hand-dug holes in the clay,
Through the treacherous grain up the rising plain
To Malon and La Folie.

Who will forget the Falaise gap?
Or Pinon west of the Orne?
But at Auchie and Gruchy, and Franqueville
Were these later victories born.

Great cities and countries have fallen now
To hosts this vanguard led.
Let us not forget the debt we owe

To the oft unhonoured dead.
I have seen the hell where a hundred fell
At Rots and Grey Le Vey,
Midst the reeking corn all mortar torn
From Gazelle to Carpiquet.
Les Buissons is the resting place
Of men who cannot die,
Glengarrians, Novas, Camerons,
Hussars and H. L. I.
They learned to fight 'midst the fetid stench,
At Buron and Periers,
They pitted their youth 'gainst the war-learned craft
Of the Panzer Grenadiers.

So honour the men of the western plains,
Black Devils, Reginas too;
The Queens, North Shores and Chaudières,
And Scots from the Western blue.
Victoria, Winnipeg, Ottawa
Sent sons for the treacherous trail,
Who must feed the guns and the tanks and the men,
The men who dare not fail.
There were gunners and sappers from homes which range
From the east to the setting sun,
And many lie where the ripening rye,
Danced to the devil's fun.
They do not ask a golden casque,
Or a tower of graven stone,
But that men may live in a world set free
From guilt by their blood atoned.

Dip gently your scythe, good reaper now
O'er the fields of the hallowed dead,
For young men fought and young men died
Near the sea, where the earth is red.

H/Capt. Stanley E. Higgs
Belgium: Vol. II, No. 31, pg. 4   *October 21, 1944*

To Those Who Fly

Hail! Lordly monarchs of the sky.
How well and proudly do you fly.
Your engines roar, your wings expand
In readiness to lend a hand.

I watch you go, I watch you come
When night is here, and day is done.
I see the marks you leave behind;
Real havoc in the Jerry's mind.

When soldiers, sailors and marines
Combine to paint the victory scenes,
You shall be there to take your place
With all who bagged the ''master race.''

Live on, ye monarchs of the sky
Good fortune be forever nigh.
The job you do is sure well done;
Let's carry on 'til all is won.

Cpl. J. A. Liverpool

Belgium: Vol. II, No. 43, pg. 4   *November 4, 1944*

Eyes Heavenward

This is my prayer, breathed from the heart
As here I stand, mud-stained and weary
In a land not mine.
Moving to the Whims of Destiny
Born of an aimless union with two clashing thoughts
Which in their time have grown too great for me,
Shorn me of every conviction except that I am right
To groan "This is my fight", and stay in foreign places
Till there's an end of it.

Make me this night a thing apart
From all this mad cacophony of sound
That tears the mind from that which he would dream of
When the Star of the East is at its height.

Cause me to tremble never more
At hated sounds of hate itself
Screaming through the night that should
Of all nights be serene,
Starbright, not lit by winged Death
Making sacrilegious noises in its whining flight.

And when I have done my part, and spanned
My spell of service in places I can never grow to love
Carry me then over the windswept, wide and clean
Expanse of ocean to the place that is my life.

R. Poulton

Italy: Vol. III, No. 25, pg. 5.   *December 23, 1944*

Going West

The battle has just ended,
Everything is quiet and still
Except the heart that beats within
The wounded soldier on the hill.

His eyes are facing Heaven,
Warm blood flows through his hair,
With the remaining strength within him
He murmurs this simple prayer:

"Forgive me, Lord, for killing men
And for the hate within me, too.
Forgive them that wounded me,
For they know not what they do."

Jack Semezuk

Italy: Vol. III, No. 31, pg. 15.   *January 1, 1945*

Belgium

A Belgium, fair, ill fated land,
Whom German hordes did twice o'er-run;
Who silent bore the heavy hand
Of occupation, life undone;
Where four long years the spark of hope
Kept burning bright 'mid foreign foes;
Where underground your men did cope
With brutal beasts by mortal blows:
Where courage never failed or fled;
Where hate has simmered to a boil;
Where untold martyrs, heroes bled
Until the freeing of your soil.

There find we welcome at your gate,
We soldiers of a foreign land;
Who in abeyance long did wait,
So far from fair, familiar, strand.
We came to uproot rotted weeds,
In Belgium planted breadth and span.
Applaud ye not, praise not our deeds;
We did our task for God and man.

Cpl. Forer

Belgium: Vol. II, No. 119, pg. 2   February 3, 1945

Unknown

'Neath a mound of earth in Italy
Where once the wheat was sown,
Lies the body of a soldier,
Marked on his cross unknown.

He was a mother's pride and joy,
Her comfort when full grown,
This son who sleeps in Italy
'Neath the cross that's marked unknown.

His life he gave up for loved ones,
Tho' his name's not carved on stone,
Still he'll never be forgotten,
Tho' his cross be marked - -unknown.

Ray

Italy: Vol. III, No. 66, pg. 4   *February 10, 1945*

In Norman Fields

In Norman fields our gallant comrades lie,
Where once, in thousands, valiantly they stood
And fought that liberty may never die--
And challenged those who said one day it would.

To France they came, our brothers, fathers, sons;
From city, farm and prairie, soldiers all;
And shed their blood beneath the tyrant's guns
To answer their beloved country's call.

But shed no tears for them, nor tend their graves.
But rather, let the Norman blossoms fade
If we who live on will not be as brave
In peace, in truth, in sacrifice well-made.

Dvr. Joseph Kelly

Belgium: Vol. II, No. 155, pg. 2   March 17, 1945

Tribute

To the fighting men of Canada
I dedicate this rhyme.
To those who fight with ''Tommy''
Along the Western Line.

To those who fly the bombers
That give the Nazis hell;
To those who sail the ocean;
They'll all have tales to tell.

Tales of deeds and daring,
Of bitterness and strife;
Of lonely nights in trenches;
It's not a happy life.

So to the men of Canada
I give my thanks sincere,
And pray that God may guide you
Safely through the year.

Bdr. J. Brennan

Belgium: Vol. III, No. 17, pg. 4   April 14, 1945

Onward[10]

From the southern shores of England
To the battle fields of France
We fought with valiant courage
Our prestige to enhance.

From Neuport on to Beveland,
Through flooded quagmire fought.
The opening up of Antwerp
That was our only thought.

In the mud and slush of Holland
We planned a deadly blitz,
In one last mighty effort
For the downfall of old Fritz.

We're heading for the Rhineland
And we're fighting now for keeps.
We'll teach to him the proverb
That what he sows, he reaps.

Our esprit de corps is in us;
We're proving who we are.
The pride of all of Canada
The fighting SSR.

Pte. Mycock

Belgium: Vol. III, No. 17, pg. 4   April 14, 1945

London - 1945

Bastion of Wondrous Isle,
Capital of freedom's world,
Finished now your years of trial
Europe's battle flags are furled.

Centuries of hard won glory,
Doubled in a half decade.
Not a page of history's story
Equals yet the stand you made.

Remember if you count the price
Of death and darkness, bomb and fire,
That your ghastly sacrifice
Kindled well the Teuton's pyre.

Mourn not the past, have no lament,
Proudly show your battle scars.
They are eternal monument
To your triumph over Mars.

G. T. H.

W. Europe: Vol. III, No. 53, pg. 4   May 26, 1945

The Redeemed

I saw him pass from the busy press
On a downtown street in his battle dress,
Swinging his arms as he marched along,
Whistling the "Beer Barrel Polka" song.

Head held high and the rhythmic beat
Of his hob-nailed boots on the busy street,
Steady his eye, his face of tan,
And I knew my country had made a man.

I thought of his years just after school,
When his only ambition was dice and pool.
Then later a date with Jigger Bug Jane;
Poker and dice, the suckers' game.

And I thought of our leaders of bygone years,
Raving of freedom, their dreads and their fears;
Of teaching boys war, forbidding them drill,
Claiming it gave them the lust to kill.

And our boys were denied, "Oh, God, the sin,"
To walk in order and discipline.
So our worthless lads just joined the gang
While our preachers preached and the churchbells rang.

And our ladies' club, I can hear them yet
Condemning with horror the School Cadet,
And mounting the pacifists' tiresome prate,
Of a uniform, teaching our boys to hate.

But let's not forget, we all share the blame,
For neglecting youth, and a nation's shame.
So today he passed, and he will never guess
How splendid he looked in his battle dress.

Swinging his arms as he passes on by,
Whistling his song, with his head held high.

Marching to glory, with a rifle and kit,
One of a million to do his bit.
I stood out there with my shoulder straight,
'Till he passed from sight, through the station gate.
And perhaps he'll come back when the battle is won,
Praise be to God, my son, my son.

J. R. W.

W. Europe: Vol. III, No. 95, pg. 4   July 14, 1945

Tribute

All these who were young have found eternal youth,
Who were so brave know valor's just reward;
Who smiling died, nor, if asked in truth
Feared the last hour, or even greatly cared.
Their hearts were always quick to love and laughter;
Happy they trod the highest peaks of life;
For them no dulling age shall follow after.
They only found escape from death in strife.

Not the slow certainty of doom for these,
Nor the long, dreary, worried hours of care;
The best of life was theirs, free from the fears,
The compass of hours... Not on bent knees
With tears mourn for those who lived and died so fair,
But bravely, smiling, remembering down through the years.

W/O J. D. Ord

W. Europe: Vol. III, No. 119, pg. 4   August 11, 1945

Fall in The Poets

The cut of the cards may not label you bards
But you're human, and Spring is in season.
Like Edgar A. Guest, have a go, do your best
To pen lines with a rhyme and a reason.

No don't quibble, men, just take up a pen
And give us full vent from your passion.
If good, you'll make hay, like E. St. V. Milay--
Try a verse with the touch Ogden Nash-on.

Perhaps you've a style somewhat like Ernie Pyle,
Or your lines may not be worth a hell, yet,
As thoughts become darker, remember Dot Parker--
Someday you'll outdo T. S. Eliot.

Don't ever refuse to pursue the old muse
With the thought that you never may see
All your efforts turn out, despite a fierce bout,
Into poems as nice as a tree.

For those who take time, to find words that will rhyme,
Here's a tip that provides you the key--
They say ours is Freedom--so why don't you heed 'em
And write verses in a style that--while not strictly
according to Hoyle is nonetheless passable and a
damned sight easier if you have scan-trouble--is free?

A. P. McGinnis

Italy: Vol. I, No. 83, pg. 5   *May 13, 1944*

II

Fear & Death

Prayer Before Battle[3]

When beneath the rumble of the guns,
I lead my men against the Huns;
It's then I feel so all alone; weak and scared,
And oft I wonder how I dared
Accept the task of leading men.

I wonder, worry, fret, and then... I pray;
O God, who promised oft
To humble man, to lend an ear;
Now, in my troubled state of mind,
Draw near, Oh God, draw near, draw near.

Make me more willing to obey,
Help me to merit my command,
And if this be my fatal day
Reach out, O God, Thy helping hand
And lead me down that deep, dark vale.

These men of mine must never know
How much afraid I really am!
Help me to lead them, in the fight,
So they will say... "He was a man."

Maj. Alex. R. Campbell

December 25, 1943

For the Fallen

Let's bow our heads and say a prayer
For the lonely grave that lies out there
Beside the road that winds and twists
Through bleak Italian rains and mists.

Beneath that solitary mound - -
Beneath that lonely, muddy ground
There lies a form that used to be
A brave Canadian, proud and free.

Pray for him who lies alone,
Pray for him who won't go home,
Pray for him, who had to die,
And ask our Lord the reason why.

Forgive us, Lord, the men who doubt
And ask you what it's all about.
Keep an eye on that lonely mound - -
It never moves, nor makes a sound.

And when the rest of us go home,
Tell us that he's not alone
Beside the road that winds and twists
Through bleak Italian rain and mists.

J. G. G.

Italy: Vol. I, No. 83, pg. 5   *May 13, 1944*

The Lonely Cross

I looked at a cross which marked a grave;
'Twas only of wood and told nothing save
That a soldier's life had passed away--
Just a cross on a grave down Sangro way.

No words were on that wooden cross,
To guess who it was, I was at a loss.
Some poor devil got it, I heard fellows say--
Just a cross on a grave down Sangro way.

Might have been a friend, perhaps even a foe;
Funny how thoughts about those things go.
May have been someone I'd met one day,
'Neath that cross on a grave down Sangro way.

So I lingered a moment and offered a prayer
For the soldier who'd found his last resting place there;
And I'll never forget it where ever I stray--
Just a cross on a grave down Sangro way.

L. S. Eckardt

Italy: Vol. I, No. 77, pg. 5   *May 16, 1944*

Slit Trench Soliloquy

When I am in the front line
And shells go whistling by,
I've often said to myself--
I'd sooner live than die.

E. J. Caughty

Italy: Vol. I, No. 107, pg. 5   June 10, 1944

For Blake

Your day was brief, the sun you hardly knew,
Cool, morning air of youth your lungs inhaled;
You walked the forenoon earth, still damp with dew,
Knew not the world that later hours regaled.

For those whom God decreed should still remain
To witness sunrise, sunset, night and day,
Night's calm nor daylight's warmth shall quell the pain
Of knowledge that a friend has passed away.

G. W. Powell

Italy: Vol. I, No. 107, pg. 5   *June 10, 1944*

The Bombed City[5]

I have seen my sons go marching
to many an alien war,
While the women wept behind them and
the gay bands played before;
Scornful if they were pitied,
with a song they went away,
They with the shining morning eyes
that scarce had seen the day.

And the grey years passed and they came again,
triumphal flags unfurled...
And my heart cried out to the unreturned
on the other side of the world.

Why now should I mourn that the scars of war
on my own broad bosom fall?
What matters it if my body be torn
when my spirit is grown so tall?
So pity me not that my homes are dark and
my streets are empty of mirth...
I am one at last with my fallen sons
in every part of the earth.

James Parish

Italy: Vol I, No. 107, p. 5   *June 10, 1944*

War

Shell-torn buildings line the sky,
Twisted trees waiting to die.
Pain-wracked bodies lying stark,
Flares and shellfire in the dark,
Unearthly wails and hideous moans,
A mortally wounded stirs and groans.
Slimy craters and splintered rocks,
Out in the dark a sniper stalks.
The air is filled with a tiger's roar
Clearing its throat of a clot of gore.
Hollow-eyed men strew the ground,
Dazed and battered by continual sound.
Shouts and screams, machine guns' rattle,
Never was there such a battle!
The night has ended, the day begun,
The objective reached, the fight is won.
The heads are counted, prayers are said,
Graves are dug for the scattered dead.
A letter home to hide a tear,
''Don't worry folks, all's quiet here''.

L/Cpl. G. S. Sheils

Italy: Vol. II, No. 96, pg. 5   *October 21, 1944*

Battleground[9]

The dead were always there,
Lying like driftwood on a shore;
Limbs awry, mouths agape, eyes staring.
We walked with care around them,
And turned our heads away.

We steeled our hearts
Striving to remember those we knew,
Those who had been full of talk and
hope and life
And not mere shattered husks
Left behind in an alien land.

We talked of other things,
To drive cold fear from our hearts;
Fear of a fate unkind as theirs,
Which might befall at any time.

And as we left the saddening sight,
Glancing backward through the dusk,
We prayed to our separate gods above
To see us safely through the night.

Robert Gray

October 25, 1944

Hold High The Torch

O, valiant hearts of yesteryear,
that sleep in Flanders Fields.
We are the dead that caught the torch
that failing hands did fling
And held it high with His own help
amidst the battle's sting.
Arise, brave warriors from thy sleep
and take us by the hand.
Strange warriors we, that needs must sleep
far from our native land.

What say ye now, O soldiers bold,
did we break faith or not?
And will our slumbers be like yours,
broken by sound of shot?
Like you we gave our all that
freedom might still reign,
That the shadows of war might never
darken our fair and wide domain.

Cpl. B. C. Maidens

Belgium: Vol. II, No. 79. pg. 4   December 16, 1944

Old Year and New

The Year dies silently
Swiftly;
Dies with its dreams,
And, perchance, desires
To heap on fires
Of war and hate.
Its fate, perhaps,
Who pauses at the door
And knocks
Then slowly moves on
Towards another year.

Another year
Of fear
And terror and heart-rending loneliness?
Torn from the depths
Of destruction
And ruin,
The days fall from the calendar
Like leaves
In autumn wind
Leaving behind
The horrid memory of the days now dead.

Pte. S. R. MacDonald

Belgium: Vol. II, No. 90, pg. 4   December 30, 1944

41

The Four Horsemen of Apocalypse

The Four Horsemen of the Apocalypse
Do their duty well,
Spreading plague and destruction,
Until to live is to be in Hell.
Riding, ever riding
They, their innocent victims seek;
Searching, ever seaching,
To slay the young, the old, the weak.
War, Death, Famine, and Disease,
Created by Man's hand;
Stalk like hideous monsters,
Laying waste the land.

What know you of the horrors of war?
And the sorrows that it brings to life,
Sitting there in a cozy chair,
By a fireside, safe from strife.
There are lands that are scorched and barren,
And as Hunger and Misery meet,
Mothers trade their honour
That their children still may eat.
The price of a maiden's virtue
Is no longer a marital vow.
Food, shelter and clothing
Are all the requirements now.
Hope has long since departed,
Despair has taken its place.
Worry and fear for the future
Is seen in each person's face.
Let us, when we count our blessings,
Think, then, of the victims of war,
And pray for the coming of peace on earth
When the Horsemen shall ride no more.

G. R. S.

Italy: Vol. III, No. 48, pg. 5   *January 20, 1945*

Sacrifice

The boy lay in the German mud.
His uniform was soaked in blood.
There wasn't anything to say,
So silently we turned away.

He used to talk a lot of home;
The Rockies and their snow-capped dome.
He loved the view at Lake Louise,
The quiet waters and the trees.

He knew the prairies, vast and wide;
The rippling wheat fields were his pride.
He loved the thunder, loud and deep;
Niagara; majestic, steep.

He loved the streets of Montreal;
The hurry, bustle, noise and all.
He loved the misty Maritimes;
The ocean and their changing climes.

He loved the same as you and I,
And for his love he chose to die.
The things he loved, no more he'll see,
But for his sacrifice, would we?

J. M. P.

Belgium: Vol. III, No. 6, pg. 2   March 31, 1945

They Sleep

A mounded plot with crosses decked
In all their earthly outward pride;
They sleep in death, as once in life,
With hero comrades, side by side.

Then sleep! Ye brave, in peace and calm,
Where God's own birds their anthems sing;
Where nature's blossoms waft their spring.
The cause is just, 'tis now secure;
No mortal power can e'er retract;
The blood you spilled, the blot too pure
Finds substance in established fact.

Sleep on, ye great! The nation's thought
Will cherish till man's breath departs,
The price you paid, the prize you bought
Enshrined in loved ones' aching hearts.

Gnr. Gill Parr

W. Europe: Vol. III, No. 47, pg. 4   May 19, 1945

Almighty And All Present Power[2]

Almighty and all present power.
Short is the prayer I make to thee;
I do not ask in battle hour
For any shield to cover me.

The vast unalterable way,
From which the stars do not depart,
May not be turned aside to stay
The bullet flying through my heart.

I ask no help to strike my foe;
I seek no petty victory here;
The enemy I hate, I know
To thee is dear.

But this I pray, be at my side,
When death is drawing through the sky;
Almighty Lord, who also died
Teach me the way that I should die.

F/O E. R. Davey, R.C.A.F.

W. Europe: Vol. III, No. 55, pg. 2   May 29, 1945

45

Progress

A misty morning, yesterday.
In earnest, or perhaps in play,
The gods arose and then began
A sad mistake; created man.

This man, at first, a quadruped,
From tree-top food until he found
That better things were on the ground.

By noon that day this man had changed,
His cities built, his life arranged.
The mists had cleared, the sun did shine,
The gods, pleased, murmured, ''This is fine.''

By night the scene had changed again,
And busily men were killing men.
When atom bombs blew all away,
The gods said, ''Well, some other day.''

Gnr. D. L. Sinclair

W. Europe: Vol. III, No. 130, pg. 4 August 25, 1945

III

Daily Living/DailyThoughts

Nightwatch On The Channel Coast[1]

Dark and the wind stirring, the clouds blown
Ragged, the surging sea.
The stamp of hobnailed boots, passing and one lone
seagull wandering free
High over the cliff-tops, wandering, calling, calling,
The tired wind sighing, on the waters, a lost star falling.

Alberta Prairies

Dusty, dead-golden, deserted the prairies lie
Under the brilliant swerve of a soulless sky...
I may never gather the harvest again, before I die.

S. J. Dowhan

From ''The Leaves are Scattered''

Italy: Vol. III, No. 33, pg. 2   January 3, 1944

Service Customs Taught to Nurses

A nurse's life with learning's rife
She must know all the answers
From pharmacy to surgeon's knife,
From tummy ache to cancers.

Sulfonamides and germicides
She knows like a brother;
Why paranoics are suicides,
Why brides go home to mother.

But studies new she must pursue,
(Their numbers quite unnerve us)
For now, 'tis ruled, she must know, too,
The Customs of the Service.

Should port be passed to left or right?
And when are side arms carried?
Can Union Jacks be flown at night?
Are all Trained Soldiers married?

Dear girls in blue, we weep for you.
Frustration is all that you borrow.
For though today you may learn something new,
It will be amended tomorrow.

Anonymous

Italy: Vol. 1, No. 35, pg. 4   March 18, 1944

Blame it on The Mud

If you're ever short an alibi and
worried as the deuce
And get that awful feeling that
your neck is in a noose
Especially here in Italy there
is always an excuse;
You can always put the blame
upon the mud!

You'll be feeling plumb disgusted and
your head is bent with woe,
While the weather--far from freezing--
feels like twenty-five below.
If the cooks have fed you bully-beef
for three meals in a row;
You can always put the blame
upon the mud.

M. St. C. Sterling

Italy: Vol. I, No. 35, pg. 5   *May 6, 1944*

The Hero of Snaffle

He's Captain Cook of the L.A.D.,
The Master of Mach'nery;
He pats each hornet's noble flank,
To him a tank is not a tank
But thing of purest ray serene
With heart and soul and bowels and spleen.

His gentle hand slips through her guts
And fondly fingers bolts and nuts;
His eyes light with unholy glee
When it's found perfect as can be.
'Tis then of bliss, he drains the cup--
"Turn over, dear, we're starting up."

G. R. H. Ross

Italy: Vol. 1, No. 83, pg. 5   *May 13, 1944*

Night on the Battle Lines

The sun in splend'rous loveliness
declines in flaming glow
And seems to pause, as to caress
the mountains, tipped with snow.
Then softly, slowly sinks away,
while waning daylight clings
'Til twilight meets the closing day
and night descends on wings.

As though released from closed-in walls
the warning zephyrs blow,
While all-enfolding darkness falls,
enshrouding earth below.
'Till, to oppose invading night,
reluctant heavens shine,
As starlight pours its feeble light
upon the battle line.

M. St. C. Sterling

Italy: Vol. I, No. 83, pg. 5   *May 13, 1944*

Homeward Flight

Through the night, towards the dawn.
The scattered squadrons fly
Proud and swift and beautiful,
Against the flame-flushed sky.

On edges of the morning,
As stars grow softly pale,
A company of warriors
Upon the homeward trail,

Below the fields of Europe--
A wrinkled map outspread,
England somewhere in the mist--
A sea of cloud ahead.

Battle-scarred, their tasks accomplished
And their duty done--
On their wings the sudden glory
Of the rising sun.

C. Callan

Italy: Vol. I, No. 89, pg. 5 May 20, 1944

Thoughts in Hospital

Italia's skies are blue and clear,
A shade of opalescent;
The lark in sheer abandon there
So blithely sings,
In Italy.

Her fields be-decked with poppies red,
With marigold and daisy;
Her vineyards, wheat fields, streams and hills,
So lovely now,
In Italy.

Not long ago the guns were heard
And gallant men fell bravely;
The youth of Canada's fair land
So fiercely fought,
In Italy.

A modern Florence Nightingale,
In khaki clad so neatly,
With patient mien, with cheerfulness,
So nobly serves
In Italy.

With quiet step and touch so sure,
She goes about her duties,
Her face is calm, so unperturbed,
Gently she smiles,
In Italy.

As dedicated spirits, we
Each duty face sincerely;
We'll seek to keep alive the flame
So brightly burned
In Italy.

A. E. Larke
Italy: Vol. I, No. 119, pg. 5　　　*June 24, 1944*

Letter to "Andy"

Dear Sir, with pleasure we report
Of recent action here,
And also feats of brothers, friends,
'Though in a different sphere.
Our present leaders, able, tough,
With us, have won acclaim;
In Italy, in Normandy,
Results have been the same.
The Hun is being driven back,
He knows not where to turn.
(Recalling days of '40, Sir,
It's nice to see him squirm).
The battle's far from over
But we're keen to play our part;
We're still the blade you termed us,
Edging close to Berlin's heart.
The tempered steel of Canada's men
Has smote the Nazi horde;
We'd like to take time out to thank
The man who forged the Sword.

J. E. C.

Italy: Vol. 1, No. 125, pg. 5   *July 1, 1944*

Beauty Abroad

The streets of Rome
Are paved,
Indeed,
With belles of ev'ry
Race and
Creed.

But just today
I saw a
Beauty--
An ATS out
Here on
Duty.

Though Roman gals
Are molta
Bella,
They don't compare
With Pte.
Stella.

W. Ealing

Italy: Vol. II, No. 18, pg. 5   July 22, 1944

Mussolini Lied

The duplicity
Of Italy
Lies in its simplicity--
It's nothing but mountains
And fountains.

R. Poulton

Italy: Vol. II, No. 36, pg. 5   August 12, 1944

Lira Lyrics

By the palazzo
Where dirty ragazzo
Squabble for cigaret butts,
And garlicky Flora,
The florid signora,
Peddles her lemons and nuts,
Lives Cici Carbone
Who runs the Salone - -
"Hey Joe, shave?"

Hurry on your way
Passing his doorway
Curtained with gaily-hued beads;
Bambini pursue you
They both cry and hue you,
Shouting your barbering needs
For Cici Carbone
Who runs the Salone - -
"Hey Joe, shave?"

In the piazza
Well-developed ragazza
Stroll, after heat of the day;
Ogling soldati
half vino-happy,
Stroll, but after their pay
Is only Carbone
Who runs the Salone - -
"Hey Joe, shave?"

If you're unbarbered,
Better stay harbored
Far from the Via Umberto;
For all of God's creatures
With bewhiskered features
There suffer this public concerto:
''Pass not the Salone
Of Cici Carbone - -
Hey Joe, shave?''

Victor Gotro

Italy: Vol. I, No. 42, pg. 5   *August 19, 1944*

Stop and Listen

Take a moment, friend or neighbor,
Passing Stranger it may be,
To consider at your leisure,
Things that shortly are to be.

War on every hand arising,
Earthquakes of tremendous force,
Ocean wrecks, with fear and bloodshed
Now seem scarcely out of course.

Are we getting harder hearted?
As we hear the awful sound of dissolving
nations crumbling?

Pte. John H. Welch

Italy: Vol. II, No. 90, pg. 5   October 14, 1944

To Their Future

What does he want who home returns?
What are the things for which he yearns?
I ask this question day by day,
And this is what they mostly say:

The loving embrace of a wife.
Little children to share their life,
A home that is in fact secure,
A peace on earth that will endure,
Time to work and time to play,
A chance to have a holiday,
The opportunity to acquire
Enough of world's goods to retire,
To live, but in a modest way,
To help some fellow every day,
And strive to build a strong foundation
For an ever-growing nation.

These are the things of which they speak,
No nobler theme could you seek.
They left as boys, now they are men,
Grant soon they may be home again.
For life and love await them there,
And no place can with Home compare.

G. R. Simpson

Italy: Vol. III, No. 1, pg. 5   November 25, 1944

Verily, A Tragedy

Their blood ran cold with horror
As they gazed on the awful scene.
Their faces pale with anguish,
And their gills turned faintly green.
For seldom has anyone suffered
As they did that horrible night.
Seldom before have humans
Beheld such a ghastly sight.
There on the ground before them
The shattered remnants lay,
And a steady stream of crimson
Seeped into the thirsty clay.
And they stood in breathless silence
As men who were stricken dumb,
For they'd just seen the sergeant-major
Break a jug of issue rum.

Sgt. D. Meade (Seaforths)

Italy: Vol. III, No. 19, pg. 5   December 16, 1944

With Each Day's Dawn

At the dawn of each day,
Just before the rising sun,
There are duties on the way,
And battle to be won.
With them comes the power
That will help us every mile,
And through each trying hour
To wear a friendly smile.
To help a weary brother
Who is bent beneath his load,
Someone perhaps none other
Had noticed up the road.

Cpr. L.T. Wilson

Belgium: Vol. II, No. 85, pg. 6   December 23, 1944

Calvados

There is a drink called Calvados,
Made in France from apples,
And when you've had a shot or two
You're ready for big battles.

For some this drink is precious stuff--
With sleep and eats it rates.
It is the finest stuff on earth
Say many of my mates.

It makes a cold chap nice and warm,
And knocks some warm chaps cold.
It leaves some strong chaps weak next day
And makes some weak ones bold.

The Tommy likes his glass of beer,
Some yanks their gin and cocktails,
But ask a Canuck just what he'll have,
And "Calvados," he wails.

Before the chaps had found this drink
Their drink was apple cider.
And now they're drinking apples still,
But Calvados, not cider.

F. W. M.

Belgium: Vol. II, No. 43, pg. 4   November 4, 1944

The Children[8]

No lion and eagle battle joy, no dust
Of horsemen streaming pennants in the park,
Nor shining swords, not spears, nor flags, but rust
And Death's great mass production leaves war's mark
Across the fields of France today. ''Long Toms''
Hurls thunder at the wind. As shrapnel falls
A sad-eye child stares at her blasted dolls
And wonders at the meaning of the bombs,
Yet not afraid, but questioning. Not I,
Nor the bright feudal pageantry of yore
Can write an answer, large across the sky
To her perplexity, nor explain war
To Jeanne, whose home is rubble now: To Paul
Whose young companions answer not his call.

Sgt. J. H. Chave

Belgium: Vol. II, No. 101, pg. 2   January 13, 1945

Betty

Betty lives in Holland,
In Holland by the sea.
She's not so darned good-looking,
But she's awfully nice to me.

She comes up past my shoulder,
And oval is her face.
Her figure is quite shapely,
With nothing out of place.

I met her at the Scala
And the music was so grand.
She was the one in many
That I could understand.

Her English was nigh perfect,
Her manners were divine,
And all her faults in dancing
Were just the same as mine.

We walked back home together
And parted at the door
And only for the curfew
I would have stayed 'til four.

Pte. J. T. Condell

Belgium: Vol. II, No. 149, pg. 2   March 10, 1945

Ogden Nashiism

I like his pomes
Of pungent odour;
Though they are
Out of moder.
He has wit
That goes with humour;
That grows on you
Like a cancerous tumour.

Be it "Benjamin" or "The City,"
They all appear equally witty.
If this be an illusion of mind
Then the moral I hope to find.

I like his stuff, I know not why;
According to the brow, it is not high.
Your powers of detection
Reveal "Genealogical Reflection."

"The Life of the Party"
Is not literarily arty;
Though it has its cruder points
It creaks around poetical joints.

He pays no attention to his metre or timing,
Only concerned that the damned things are rhyming!
So if you think this sounds like Nash,
Let's convert it into ready cash.

Sgt. E. K.

Belgium: Vol. III, No. 6, pg. 2   March 31, 1945

Pinups

To pin-up girls who coyly pose
In all our daily papers
Some oppose the lack of clothes
As detrimental capers.

It seems they feel morality
Is lowered by the pinup,
And gives no sense of cheerfulness,
Nor helps me keep the chin up.

Fond mem'ries of the wife and kids,
Or of the girl back there;
They claim is driven out of mind
By the girl who poses bare.

They'd rather have the ''wholesome'' type,
Adorned in lots of stuff,
Well bedecked in silks and furs,
Face hidden by a muff.

But whether clothed or posed so chic,
A gal is just a gal,
So give us more of the pin-up type,
And to the heck with our morale.

Sgt. R. W. Evans

W. Europe: Vol. III, No. 47, pg. 4   May 19, 1945

For Herbie[11]

When old Ortona's walls and grapevines fell,
And drooping, dripping skies rained iron and rain,
Out of some nightmare's nest or padded cell,
Our Herbie sprang from Bing's bewildered brain.

Disaster dogs him. If a brick should fly
It bounces off poor Herb's resilient skull;
If hostile stonking blows the wine-keg dry,
It is before poor Herbie's mug is full;
When generals inspect us on review
His uniform is torn, and muddy too.

His many-sided personality
Reflects a little now of you, now me.
And he will stick by us to the end,
Our shovel-faced and rabbit-witted friend!

Sgmn. R. H. Whittaker

W. Europe: Vol. III, No. 65, pg. 4   June 9, 1945

On Guard

Have you ever stood at a listening post
With your eyes strained into the gloom?
And you prayed with all your heart and soul
For the sight of the silvery moon?
Where at two your shift seems like half the night
As you stood there alone in the dark,
And your nerves are tense and your muscles tight
Like a cannon awaiting the spark.

Your thoughts go back to days long ago
When a night like this was a thrill,
For a Hallowe'en prank or some other stunt
You think of them all; then until--
Was that a noise and did that tree move?
Was that big rock over there before?
Did that old cross seem to move its arms?
And that log's not there anymore.

Should you shout out the password or toss a grenade
Or give it a burst with a Bren?
No! You just sit quiet and listen and look
And see if it happens again.
Then you hear it again much clearer this time,
And your heart seems full of grief.
But at last you catch on and you know what's the score,
It's only your pal, your relief.

T. H. Thompson

W. Europe: Vol. III, No. 65, pg. 4   June 9, 1945

Desperate

Everyone is restless.
We don't know what to do.
Leave for home just leaves us guessing
And it has you guessing, too.

It seems we need a Kaiser,
And we don't mean Kaiser Bill,
But the man who built the freighter
And we want him building still.

There's an ocean trip before us,
The ships are in demand
For cargoes that are headed
To the doomed land of Japan.

Kaiser's coming over,
Building houses down in France,
We have to wait some more, boys,
So just hitch up your pants.

It's no good to start crying.
There is nothing we can do.
But can anyone tell me
Where I'll find a good canoe?

Pte. J. M. Mont

W. Europe: Vol. III, No. 77, pg. 4   June 23, 1945

We Carry On

We have left you lads behind us,
We have carried on the fight.
In the heart of fortress Europe
We have smashed with Allied might.
By your glories deep inspired
We have made the West Wall dust,
And the mighty Nazi cannon
Lie corroding, thick with rust.

So the torches which you carried
When your days beside us ceased,
We now carry on to guide us
Through our battles in the East.
We recall your small white crosses
And our eyes, at times, are wet,
But we're going to keep on fighting
'Til the Rising Sun has set.

Sgmn. A. Steel

W. Europe: Vol. III, No. 77, pg. 4   June 23, 1945

The Chairborne Troops

Sure, we sat a few miles behind the guns,
We guys with the soft touch go,
And lived in comfort, without rain or slush,
Or exposed to the tempest's blow.

But did we not have it all so soft
And as cushy as you are told?
Just listen, my friend, while I put down my pen
To a story damp and cold.

Way back of the lines it wasn't so slick.
Ask any D. R. that I know.
They, too, got wet and dirty and stiff
From pounding a bike in the snow.

Sure it rained back here, and the tents all leaked,
And we also ate Compo and mush.
And we worked all night in the big top tents,
When the front moves up in a rush.

And remember ''V'' bombs that roared through the sky
With fire and noise and death?
They dropped on us in that cushy go,
And we felt the Reaper's breath.

I still say ''tops'' is the infantry,
Who smashed far into the Hun.
But remember the boys where your grub came from,
And the bullets for your gun.

And we can't wear stripes to tell of our wounds,
But there's scars a lot of us bear.
We have the marks to show, ne'er the less,
From sitting all night in our chair.

Cpl. L. Keyte

W. Europe: Vol. III, No. 95, pg. 4   July 14, 1945

The Golden Rule

Freedom of speech is a cherished aim
For which we have sought to save.
But three G. I.'s took advantage of this
In a speech they thought bold and brave.

In the F. P. O. of our Maple Leaf
Where some of us speak our mind,
They slammed and condemned our khaki girls
In a way that was far from kind.

The said they were out for a roaring good time;
Gold-diggers and officer stuff.
In wisecracks and insults they wasted no breath,
But we think they've said more than enough.

With replies from the girls standing up for their rights,
And for boys pitching in for their share.
For remember we've sisters, and sweethearts and friends,
And we're proud of the khaki they wear.

One fellow replies that they've done a swell job,
At sorting our mail for our cheer.
They love the army no more than we do,
And they'd much sooner be far from here.

You've got the wrong slant boys, I'm sorry to say,
For had you been up at the front
You'd have learned to appreciate things that are good
And forgotten your slammings so blunt.

We ourselves are not perfect, we know that is true,
So let's work on a much better plan.
Keep your own doorsteps clean and don't throw any rocks.
Be an asset, a real gentleman.

Pte. Mycock

W. Europe: Vol. III, No. 101, pg. 5   July 21, 1945

Playing The Game

It's not what we say we will do in this life.
It's not what we think or we know.
It's not just the person we think that we are.
It's the things that we do and we show.

It's not all the things that we know can be done.
It's not all our knowledge so true.
It's not all the lessons we've learned in this life.
It's the facts and the acts that we do.

It's not just the knowing of what should be done.
It's not just revealing the same.
It's doing whatever you know you should do.
It's simply called ''Playing the game.''

Kjaer Jensen

W. Europe: Vol. III, No. 113, pg. 4   August 4, 1945

Why

Why, when earth's deep stores
Offer abundant riches and wealth untold,
Does man steal the fruit of his brothers' chores?
Destroy and kill for an ounce of gold?

Why, when earth's broad face
Has won for all in which to toil,
Does man contest his brothers' place?
Destroy and kill for a foot of soil?

Why, when earth's great seas
Are so vast as to be beyond assay,
Does man seek control of his brothers' quays?
Destroy and kill for the right of way?

Shall it be so in the years we face
When the great traffic is in the sky?
Will man challenge his brothers' space,
Destroy and kill for the right to fly?

Cpl. R. A. Cater

W. Europe: Vol. III, No. 130, pg. 4   August 25, 1945

Utrecht

When you hear the name Utrecht,
Maybe you think of fighting in the square,
Wild rumours, hard words, blows, shots,
Petty things dividing us when great things
Should unite us.
I'd rather think of Paul, who offered me a painting,
Over which he'd laboured long:
"Take it with you when you go,
For your kindness." he said.
My kindness!
A few spare smokes, dark chocolate bars I never eat,
Some tins of fish from home I didn't want.
I'd rather think of Paul's wife, Frieda,
Who faithfully washed my clothes each week,
Mended each hole, replaced each button,
Cooked me lovely, golden pancakes:
A simple, kind and friendly person,
Who didn't speak my tongue,
But didn't need to.
"Frieda was something weeping," said Paul's letter,
When she heard that you may not be home for Christmas."
I'd rather think of four year old Dora.
Shy at first, but gradually making friends
And venturing to perch on "Uncle George's" knee.
"We will never forget you!" said Paul's letter.
I'll remember that
When trouble in the streets is long forgotten.

L/Cpl. G. G. Patterson

N.W. Europe: Vol. IV, No. 33, pg. 5   October 13, 1945

A German Child

Reach out dear hand and bequeath
This sullen child whose only mirth
Lies hidden lifeless beneath
A ravaged mind since birth,
That he alone may find
A patient word--a light
Of goodness overflowing the mind
Surging forth--a storming might,
Reaching the inner depths with calm,
Quelling the solid fright where
Now a smile lays hidden; a psalm
On quivering lips aware,
Of a tear's burning palm,
That came without a word or care.

Richard O'Brien

W. Europe: Vol. III, No. 119, pg. 4   August 11, 1945

Snow

It snowed last night! The tiny flakes
Fall from the heavens, over the lakes
Now frozen with splendour and glistening sheen
Like the Queen of the Night whom I've never seen.

It snowed last night, and the thought was strong,
Of the days which are passed; it seems so long.
Of the times we had in the moonbeam's glow,
When the whole of the world was covered with snow.

Pte. Jack Smith

Germany: Vol. V, No. 37, pg. 2   *December 25, 1945*

To Holland

The steady flow of years has passed us o'er.
Life marks the time on slow, relentless feet.
Familiar things we soon shall know no more:
The pat of wooden shoes on cobbled street.
The spicy smell of breezes from the sea
Shall fill the lockers of sweet memory.

Your quiet, peaceful towns we know so well:
The homely folk that claimed us as their own,
Not knowing why, but understanding still
How much it meant to have a taste of home;
With eager hands threw cottage portals wide,
Insisted that we should sit down inside.

A few short days and we are homeward bound,
Great wastes of rolling water lie between.
True loves and lasting friendships we have found,
Your steadfastness and sufferings we have seen.
We know the deeds you have so nobly done,
And thank you, we your foster sons.

Sgmn. Don Warren

Germany: Vol. V, No. 37, pg. 2   *December 25, 1945*

VI

Dreams

Soldiers May Dream

There's a trail I know through a belt of bush,
Where poplar and willow sway
And the cranberries show like a splash of flame,
Gleaming red on an Autumn day.

One day I'll wander there again,
By the bank of a Western river,
Where Nature's ways all teach the creed
That all life lives forever.

I'll catch once more in that land of peace,
Old sights and smells that I know:
The new turned furrow, the scent of spruce,
The Northern Lights aglow.

The Spring thaw, and the ploughing rain,
The ooze of April mud:
After winter's frozen fastnesses
We know that these are good.

These are the things of a soldier's dreams,
These are the things of worth.
And these shall gladden a soldier's heart,
When Peace shall fill the Earth.

Eric A. Dowson

Italy: Vol. I, No. 107, pg. 5   *June 10, 1944*

Ghosts of The Living

In these our days, I find myself a stranger;
The summers which the years divide for me
Are lived by people unconfined by danger--
With whom I left my heart when I was free.

In every haunted, tall, fantastic city,
In prairie stillness by secluded streams,
Beyond the sunset, strange to praise or pity,
Unnumbered, unlived lives remain as dreams.

Mathew Wherry

Italy: Vol. II, No. 42, pg. 5   *August 19, 1944*

The Lonesome Cowboy

It's a long way from the prairie
To a funk-hole in the mud,
From the mesquite and the sagebrush
To this agony of blood.
For the howling of the coyotes,
Is replaced by grimmer sounds
And the vast expanse of mesa
Is defaced by man-made mounds.

But I'll keep my dreams before me
Through this carnival of hell,
Though its hard to keep the memory
Of sage and chapparal.
And when the show is over
I'll be riding as before,
O'er the wide unbounded prairie,
And I'll leave it nevermore.

S/Sgt. F. J. Nethercut

Belgium: Vol. II, No. 13, pg. 4   September 30, 1944

Just For Today

Dream not of days that used to be,
Or skies of blue that now are gray,
Those joys and troubles once we knew
Have vanished now, and passed away.

Another day is yet to come;
And those before, alas, have gone.
Why worry over something lost,
Or something we have never known.

There is no yesterday, my dear.
There's no tomorrow, just today.
Let's snatch our share of joy and life
And happiness while yet we may.

S/Sgt F. J. Nethercut

Belgium: Vol. II, No. 25, pg. 4   *October 14, 1944*

A Canuck In Italy[6]

Death, gloating in its shroud, did cover me,
Tempting my tired soul to gain its rest.
"Rise from this wet and mud-bound sea,
What matters if you fall--to gain the crest?"

Crawling, stumbling, blindly falling,
Groping for the top.
For what, you idiotic fool? Does rest deter you not?
Is not this pain, the price that greed has wrought?
Why struggle on to lose that which you sought?

Then light! Oh brilliant, dazzling beam!
You spectrum of a soldier's dream,
Bursting forth to free my soul,
Through closed, pink lids I saw my goal.

Excelling all in simplicity
Stood Christ on a cross--humanity.

Anonymous

Italy: Vol. II, No. 108, pg. 5   *November 4, 1944*

That Little Land

I sat on the stone of a terrace wall
Hearing the noise great and small;
The distant clock, a nearer tone
Of the sentry's feet on the cobblestones,
The drone of an aeroplane overhead,
A bird song from a cactus bed.
I saw the bird with its ruddy breast,
An English robin I almost guessed.
Then my heart went back to the Surrey hills,
The silent pools, the water mills,
A hamlet sleeping in the sun,
Creeping dusk when the day is done,
The firelight on two faces small
Watching shadows on the wall,
The nights I carried the two to bed
Tucked them in and sometimes read
Of fairy princes and pretty queens
Until they entered the land of dreams.
Here I am 'neath a Southern sky,
The minutes and hours drifting by.
But I wish for England's damp and chill
For half my heart is in England still.

Forwarded by Cpl. Wheelock

Italy: Vol. III, No. 13, pg. 5   *December 9, 1944*

Before The Zero Hour

Just one more night that seemed the same
As hundreds gone before
Yet, somehow different.
The tension seemed to freeze men to the core.
A star shell burst with all the
glory of the sun.
Crouching men trembled, but knew better
than to run.
In ditches, where the shadows and the
bushes hid them well,
In trenches and in shell-holes and in
every nook and dell
They waited.
And there, nerves were drawn so tight and grim,
They whispered some in curses,
Some trying to think of Him.
Their loved ones, wives and sweethearts,
Seemed so close there in the night,
Seemed to smile, and smiling
Tell them to carry on the fight;
Seemed to say, "We're waiting for you.
Please hurry and come back.
Our spirits will stay with you
Through the bullets and the flak."
The visions fade; the forbidding night
Closes all around.
Once more they will wait in silence,
lying on the muddy ground.
Then a flash, like brilliant lightning,
And a roar they knew so well--
The Zero Hour has come at last,
As the guns unleash their hell.

Pte. M. D. Munro

Italy: Vol. III, No. 78, pg. 4   February 24, 1945

Last Night I Dreamed

I saw it there, so close it seemed,
that cottage by the sea.
It nestled there among the pines.
Close by there seemed to be
The same old garden, roses sweet,
their fragrance in the air.
The small green fence, with its white-
washed gate; the same worn path was there.

The years were bridged as I stood and looked.
So real and alive it seemed.
'Twas nice to be home after all this time.
But then, last night I dreamed.

The tools of war were put away.
No guns, no tanks, no planes.
The noise of battle had lost itself
'mid quiet country lanes.
No tramp of feet, no crash of guns,
no lorries rolling by;
Just a quiet peace, the grass, the trees,
and a breeze which seemed to sigh.

Yet when I stood beside the gate,
And the moonlight softly gleamed.
I knew the time would come again,
Because last night, I dreamed.

Sgt. C. W. MacDougall

Belgium: Vol. II, No. 13, pg. 4   September 30, 1944

Shadows

Dark shadows of the trees now bare of leaves,
Fall o'er the pathway in the moonbeam's light;
Dark shadows that are trees, but now might be
A hundred crosses standing in the night.

Pale moon that casts the shadows o'er the road
Cares not for thoughts which might assail the mind.
She rides the clouds and beckons to each star,
And hastens from the sun which lies behind.

And now the crosses seem to be on fire;
A place where many a weary soldier lay.
But come! The sun has risen in the east,
And shadows flee from out the light of day.

And once again the trees stand straight and bare,
Their brances reaching to the cloudless sky.
And crosses? They have gone away with night.
'Twas just a strange illusion of the eye.

Pte. Roy Williams

Belgium: Vol. II, No. 19, pg. 4   October 7, 1944

Hitler in Hell

The other night I had a dream when
dozing for a spell.
I dreamed that Adolph Hitler died and
descended right to Hell.
And the Devil met him at the gate and
questioned him with vim
About his worldly actions and
of his many sins.

And Hitler boasted loud and long
'til almost out of breath.
He told of concentration camps,
of putting Jews to death.
He counted on his fingers 'til
he could count no more,
He told of harmless cities he had
ruined by the score.

And his chest stuck out with fiendish
pride as he told of little babes,
One day gurgling, full of life,
the next day in their graves.
He boasted of his Doodle Bugs and
other things he'd made.
Then told of shooting prisoners,
as on and on he raved.

He told about his aide de camp
but omitted Rudolph Hess.
He claimed that Mussolini was
just a no good pest.
He lauded long on Himmler, on
Goering, "Mighty Flyer",
And not forgetting Goebbels,
the world's most famous liar.

Then the Devil called his warden, saying,
"Bring me all the keys.
And bring me all the plans of Hell
along with all the fees.
And pack up all my baggage,
for I'm leaving for a spell,
To seek a new location and
start another Hell."

And turning to poor old Hitler and said,
with no offence,
"The keys and all that Hell contains
are yours from this day, hence,
For one as cruel as you are,
yet lived the tale to tell,
You're a damn sight worse than I am,
and deserve a proper Hell."

Bdr. E. G. Jeffery

Belgium: Vol. II, No. 67, pg. 4   December 2, 1944

The Vision

I looked afar across the sea,
A vision there appeared to me;
A vision of the one I love,
Who seemed to pray to God above.

A vision seemed to me so near,
My thoughts gave way to troubled fear.
A vision of the one so dear
Who reared me from a child.

To curb my fears I found no way,
No sleep for me at the end of the day.
It kept returning to my mind'
No healthful answer can I find.

Until I hear the bugle's note,
My fears are gone, my trouble smote.
I realize, I've been the goat.
I find I've only dreamed.

Pte. P. Tompkins

W. Europe: Vol. III, No. 101, pg. 5   July 21, 1945

My Dream

I had a lovely dream last night
While I was fast asleep.
I dreamed that we were sailing
Across the briny deep.

Four days we had been sailing,
And everyone was gay,
For we knew we would be docking
Within another day.

The tugboat came to meet us,
And they threw us up a rope.
They seemed so glad to see us
That it brightened up our hope.

They pulled us tight into the dock
And dropped the gang-plank down.
Then proudly down it did we walk
To that little eastern town.

The band was playing loudly
And we didn't mind the rain.
We marched past very proudly
And climbed aboard the train.

We rolled by lake and river,
Across the mountains too.
Until we reached Vancouver
Where I knew that I'd see you.

I held you close to kiss you,
Your eyes were looking up.
I placed my arms around you,
And then I wakened up.

But that's the way with every dream
When you reach the better part.
I know not why, but it always seems
You wake up with a start.

But do not give up hoping.
This dream will soon come true,
And I shall soon be sailing
Across the sea to you.

Sgt. O. C. Graham

W. Europe: Vol. III, No. 113, pg. 4   August 4, 1945

V

Hope

Ode to Unsung Poets

What talent undiscovered lies
Beneath the warrior's lowering brow,
What gentle wit, what thought so wise,
Becomes apparent to us now.

For spring her hand hath softly laid
On those who'll hear her whispered news,
The man of steel and tender maid
Set out to woo the ancient muse.

Fill up, fill up the flowing bowl
And then with Omar drain the can,
Unloose the pent-up flow of soul
And gambol with the godless Pan.

Let spring her fires within you light
And may you see in your brimming glass
See lines you ne'er before could write
And glimpses of a favourite lass.

G. R. H. Ross

Italy: Vol. I, No. 77, pg. 5   May 6, 1944

Source of Strength

Whence comes our strength to live and fight,
And face monotony of war?
What changes doubtful dawn to light
And gives us will to do yet more?

The choking dust, the burning heat.
The ever-present threat of death:
The stench, the blood, no quiet retreat.
All threaten our desire for breath.

Then comes the balm, the healing cup
To smooth away the lines of hate,
The little note that cheers us up
And tells us "courage dear, we wait".

The news from home, those precious lines.
From loved ones many miles away
Instills our weary, tattered minds
With courage for another day.

G. H. Adlam

Italy: Vol. I, No. 107, pg. 5   *June 10, 1944*

Do You Wonder

Do you wonder that the sky is blue,
The foliage green, the birds that fly
From tree to tree the whole day through,
Despite the guns that roar nearby?

Do you wonder why the children play
Amidst the rubble of the street,
While oxen grope their lazy way,
And sheep repeat their mournful bleat?

Do you wonder why love is so strong,
Between the lover and his maid
In such a world which has gone wrong,
Where human nature is betrayed?

Do not wonder. 'Tis God's plan.
War cannot kill those good desires,
Which are the heritage of man,
And shall outlast all proud empires.

Man's spirit shall remain the same,
Despite the ruins of fire and sword;
Man shall win back his place again.
Oh, haste the day, we pray Good Lord.

J. M. C.

Italy: Vol. II, No. 12, pg. 5   *July 15, 1944*

Sick Of It

So you're sick of the way the country's run,
And you're sick of the way the rationing's done,
And you're sick of standing around in line.
you're sick, you say. Well, ain't that fine?
For I am sick of the sun and the heat,
And I'm sick of the feel of my aching feet,
And sick of the siren's wailing shriek,
And I'm sick of the groans of the wounded and weak.
I'm sick of the slaughter, I'm sick to my soul,
I'm sick of playing the killer's role,
And I'm sick of the groans of death and the smell,
And I'm sick, damned sick, of myself as well.
But I'm sicker still of the tyrant's rule,
And conquered lands where the wild beasts drool
And I'm cured damned quick when I think of the day
When all this hell will be out of the way;
When none of this mess will have been in vain,
And the lights of the world will blaze again,
And the Axis flags will be dipped and furled,
And God looks down on a perfect world.

Craig Heath

Italy: Vol. II, No. 18, pg. 5   *July 22, 1944*

Peace In War

It's peaceful in the twilight
As the shades of eve come down,
And all is hushed and quiet
Throughout the mountain town.

There is something 'bout this hour,
Controlled by God's own hand,
As though to bring a spell of peace
To a heaving, shell-rocked land.

The dogs of war, exhausted,
Have lain them down to rest;
'Tis the hour of the evening
That the soldier loves the best.

And sitting in the twilight
Beneath the heavenly dome,
A soldier's thoughts are not of war,
But of a far-off home.

We are thankful, Lord in heaven,
For the hour that You've set
For us to dwell on days of yore
In peace--lest we forget.

J. W. Oldford

Italy: Vol. II, No. 24, pg. 5   *July 29, 1944*

On Going Home

Sometimes I think that I would like to sail
Across the westward sea and travel home;
And find you waiting there for me.
I'd like to see the widening surge of foam
Sweep from ship's stern to make a frothy trail
From these strange shores to those I know and love;
To put behind me all this phantasy
Of man-made death--around, below, above,
And ruins everywhere; to move once more
In that small, happy world we knew,
Where everything was whole, complete; where war
Could never reach. But reason tells me true:
"The road to that world lies not to the West.
Push on! It lies beyond that shell-torn crest."

R. E. Beamish

Italy: Vol. II, No. 48, pg. 5   *August 26, 1944*

The House of Mercy

'Twas mid an ugly scene
Of earth plowed deep by howling bomb
And whistling shell,
With a background of trees
Leaves and limbs gone,
And trunk half-felled
That first I saw, as in a dream
The House of Mercy.
I breathed a sigh;
'Twas like returning home from hell.

How strange that this grey house
Now but a broken shell
Of twisted steel, burned wood and stone
That was one time, I feel,
To some poor soul a place called home,
Should kindle in my breast
A spark of hope
And whisper to my mind
"Fear not--you are not alone."

And yet 'twas not the sight
Alone of this gray ruin,
This utter loss,
Charred remnants here the proof.
'Twas rather in a cross
Of Red and White
Emblazoned on its roof
That I found peace,
And knowledge, too,
That soon some healing hand
Would come my pain to soothe.

J. L. A.

Italy: Vol. II, No. 54, pg. 5   *September 2, 1944*

Blow Gently, Good Wind

Blow gently, good wind, from over the sea,
Fanning the leaves of the cherry tree,
Cooling desires of the bumble bee;
Blow gently, good wind.

Over the fields of ripening grain,
Hasten the coming of cooling rain,
Whisper the hope of harvest again;
Blow gently, good wind.

Chasing the clouds over the peaks,
Where lonely monk his vigil keeps,
Down to the earth, where shepherd seeks
Solace from you, good wind.

Pausing to bless the poppies red,
Spreading their beauty over the dead,
Scattering insense over their bed;
You kind, good wind.

Blow gently, good wind, from over the sea;
How mankind longs, like you, to be free.
Your secret lies in your will to be
A gentle, good wind.

"J" (Italy, '44)

Italy: Vol. II, No. 78, pg. 5   *September 30, 1944*

"Civil Engineering"

The day is not so distant when
You'll be on civvie street again.
The time is coming when you'll be
Back with your friends and family.
So have you taken time out yet
To brush up on your etiquette?
Your manners must be polished, too,
Instead of brass and army shoe;
You're gonna find it isn't easy
Behaving like a Canadese.
For instance you must sit to eat
And through your meal you keep your seat.
Never, never, never, reach
Across the table for a peach.
Remember that a civvie lives
On butter with no adjectives.
There is no line up, no delay,
You get your meals three times a day;
When walking down the avenue
The greeting is "How do you do?"
But when an officer goes by
Just tip your hat and holler "Hi!"
Remember that the corner store
Has garden vegetables galore,
Stealing 'taters from your neighbor
Leads to six months with hard labor.
Flogging blankets is taboo--
Remember, they belong to you.
You can wave a "buona sera",
To the phoney Itie Lira;
Bid welcome to Canadian change,
Even though you'll find it strange.
Bathtubs, toilets, kitchen sinks,
Fresh cow's milk and bottled drinks,
Revolving doors and escalators,
Restaurants with aproned waiters--
A new world opens up for you,

The door is wide--and what a view!
But don't dare think it a pushover,
There's lots of weeds among the clover;
Take warning, ladies, whose hearts are yearning
For your menfolk's home returning;
Pause a while in your elation--
Prepare yourselves for transformation.

Charles King (PPCLI)

Italy: Vol. II, No. 84, pg. 5   *October 7, 1944*

Life

Life is only what you make it,
It can be as grim as death.
It can hold a world of gladness
Every time you draw a breath.

It can be a bed of roses
Or an agony of pain.
It may banish gloom and darkness
Like the sunshine after rain.

It may have its grevious troubles
And its sorrows and its cares,
Or a joy and a contentment
Which you hardly knew were there.

It can be a thing of beauty
Or a sordid thing to view.
It can be whate'er you wish it,
For the answer's up to you.

S/Sgt. F. J. Nethercut

Belgium: Vol. II, No. 43, pg. 4   November 4, 1944

Soldier's Anthem

O Canada, My Canada!
How I long to see your shore
Rise out of the sea, and grow
Till our ship, no longer large,
Slips into your welcome arms.

To feel your soil beneath my feet before
I mount an iron steed, and speed
Across your vast domain
Till I am home again
In Canada, My Canada.

Jack Semezuk

Italy: Vol. III, No. 1, pg. 5   *November 25, 1944*

The Hobo

I tramp all day
Up hill and down,
As I wander on
From town to town.

Sometimes I'm lucky,
And sometimes not.
But I get along
On what I've got.

My hair is long
And my shoes are worn.
I need a shave
And my clothes are torn.

But I've got something
I wouldn't trade
For all the finest
That's ever made.

I've got the earth
I've got the sky.
Beneath its dome
Each night I'll lie.

The moon's my lamp,
The earth's my bed.
Each night I count
The stars o'erhead.

I ask no favours
Big or small.
I care no whit
What next befall.

So you go your way
I'll go mine.
I want no pity
Anytime.

As long as there's
A moon above,
I'm clinging to
The life I love.

S/Sgt. F. J. Nethercut

Belgium: Vol. II, No. 90, pg. 4   *December 30, 1944*

That Promised Life

Lord, on earth may Thy will be done.
This day we pray for thy rising sun
When men no longer take life for life,
And nations end this bitter strife;
When hate and lust and wordly sin
Have met their death in battle's din,
And out of this crescendo of hate
There arise all that was ever great;
Love and goodwill and fellowship true,
All will survive, Lord, thanks to You.

Our sacrifice will not be in vain
When the lion with the lamb hath lain;
And all the muddling of the years
Has led us through this vale of tears
To come, oh Lord, at last to Thee
And live Thy way through eternity.
Now we look forward to that promised life
To end all want and fear and strife.
Lord, we pray for Thy rising sun,
This day on earth may Thy will be done.

John A. Rogers

Belgium: Vol. II, No. 90, pg 4   December 30, 1944

War Town

I strolled over the roof tops that lay
on the ground,
And gazed at the debris, spread all around.
Even cellars seemed lifted on high,
Naked house chimneys, looking so shy.
There stands a green house, the framework,
at least.
Look, there's a window all in one piece!
Over the rubble where once was a street,
A lone opera slipper, looking so neat.
The once joyous beer house, now full of gloom,
A wide open look of a three-sided room.
A once stately church reclines in a heap,
Why, even the dead are robbed of their sleep.
A tiny cot of some little boy,
A twisted part of his favorite toy,
The dumbfounded look of the terrified dog
As he wanders about as though in a fog.
Never a building with original shape,
Done by man who has learned to hate.
Previous cities that I have seen
Cannot compare with this horrid scene.
How quickly these cities get into this state,
Yet take so long for man to create.
Someday, maybe, peace will come,
Soldiers home and battles won.
Airmen who turned cities to dust
Hope that all war machinery will rust.
From then on it's up to you and I
To keep peace and faith in those who die.
To love, not to hate, create, not destroy.
It's all up to you, you and your boy.

Spr. J. D. Cowling

Belgium: Vol. II, No. 161, pg. 2   March 24, 1945

Beginning of Life

Far as I gazed into the heart of man
Seeking a way of life;
A life containing
Simple virtues.

The search seemed endless.
Long years I floundered
Into the depths of despair;
A ship without a course, a man
Without a soul.

The search is ours. Of that I'm sure,
For what strange notions warm the heart?
Eyes, that could not see have seen!
Ears that could not hear, have heard!
Have seen, have heard, have felt
The wonders of the world and
All they mean to me.

Alive at last, to the
Simplicity of life;
To feel a part of God's green acre.
To see within the hearts of man
The living truth of brotherhood.

Sgt. D. H. Smith

W. Europe: Vol. III, No. 83, pg. 5   June 30, 1945

Hope For Peace

I've heard the guns that roared by night,
That filled the sky with eerie light,
That belched forth flame and whining shell
And made our world a flaming Hell.

I hope and pray that nevermore
The world will hear the sounds of war.
That for all time the guns will cease
And man with man will live in peace.

I've seen my comrades lying dead
In what was not a pleasant bed;
They died in dirt, in mud, in slime,
That we may live in peace sublime.

I hope and pray that nevermore
The world will see the sights of war,
That from this strife before our eyes
A world of freedom will arise.

I've felt the moods of hate and fear,
And know too well that death was near,
That someone's husband, someone's son,
Would fall beneath the deadly gun.

I hope and pray that nevermore
The world will feel the Hate of war.
That thoughts of love we'll treasure dear,
And cleanse our hearts of hate and fear.

Pte. H. E. Parkes

NW. Europe: Vol. IV, No. 50, pg. 5   November 3, 1945

115

VI

Love

Your Friend

If he laughs when you are gay,
If he grieves when you are sad,
If he tolerates your follies
Without end.

If he makes your way his way,
If his presence makes you glad,
If he knows your faults yet loves you
He's your friend.

Anonymous

Italy: Vol. I, No. 95, pg. 5   *May 27, 1944*

Mother

There's a breathless hush in the room tonight,
There's an air-raid on, and heavens are bright,
The sky is full of smoke and planes
Shrapnel is dropping on country lanes.
The power is off, Black fills the night,
But somewhere, near me, I see a light
Your picture stands beside my bed--
A radiant halo 'round your head.

It seems to brighten up the room,
When you are near, there is no gloom,
Your picture is all I have left, you see,
But I feel that it is protecting me.

The raid is over--the light beams bright;
I kneel, and pray, with all my might;
I pray that you will ever be
There when danger threatens me.

Ernest Charles Cossar

Italy: Vol. I, No. 89, pg. 5   *May 20, 1944*

To His Mistress' Eyebrow

A ballad to your eyebrow, Fairest One?
That is the pleasant task that Shakespeare set
As one befitting lovers; therefore let
Me try my hand; it should be easily done.
Its graceful curve--that, I could dwell upon
In glowing words (if I could just forget
Those other curves, more luring, softer yet,
Which still my pen before I have begun,
With marveling); or I could haply sing
The lovely invitation it extends
When subtly lifted, save that everything
About you does invite when you're inclined.
How can I sing of what one brow portends
When all of you is so much on my mind?

R. E. Beamish

Italy: Vol. II, No. 36, pg. 5   *August 12, 1944*

Nostalgia

When do I miss you most? When evening comes
And twilight falls as gently as your touch,
While all my thoughts turn homeward in the gloom?
Or in the deep of night, when there is such
Oppressive silence that the darkness hums
With tiny sounds, inaudible by day,
And ghosts of memory march across my room?
Or in the sun-drenched morning, when clouds play
Games with the breeze that blows in from the sea;
The blue sky smiling at their childish zest
As you, my dear, have often smiled at me?
What other hours are there? Name the rest;
It matters not, for of the twenty-four,
Each passing hour I miss you that much more.

R. E. Beamish

Italy: Vol. II, No. 42, pg. 5   *August 19, 1944*

Letter From Home

(Excerpts from a letter in rhyme written to a lad in the Irish Regiment by his mother)

Again I sit down to write you a letter,
Hope you are well; we couldn't be better.
I've plenty of paper and plenty of time.
So just to be different I'll write this is rhyme.
It is Sunday and things have been quiet all day;
Shirley is here, with her father and May.
Supper is over and work is all done,
We're out in the yard watching Shirley have fun.
I think you have chosen a lovely girl, Jack,
And we'll throw a big party and have so much fun
I'll let the whole world know I'm proud of my son.
You will have the position in life that you've earned
And you'll use to advantage the lessons you've learned;
So just keep your chin up and don't you forget
There is happiness coming to all of you yet.
And there is a favour--please do it for me,
It will please me so much that I know you'll agree;
You remember the psalm that you used to recite--
"The Lord is My Shepherd"? Please say it tonight.
Say it aloud so the fellows can hear,
It will strengthen their courage and banish their fear.
By now I have written 'bout all I can write.
I think time has come that I say "Good Night."
So now that I'm finished, the letter is done;
May God bless you Jack. Loads of love from your Mom.

Anonymous

Italy: Vol. II, No. 48, pg. 5   *August 26, 1944*

To My Wife

We have forever now: Time, all the world,
Laughter and spring are ours. Each smoke-veiled dawn
And sunset's sweet, now that we can go on
In life together. Though warring flags, unfurled
Across the boiling seas defiance wave,
And cities crumble 'neath the heel of power,
When evil seems to rule the earth this hour
Our love is stronger, and such love is brave.
I'll always see you as you are tonight,
Curled by the fire, your hand upon my knee,
Reflecting in your eyes the dancing light
And play of shadow. Here is our Victory!
Our hearth inviolable, the dark days past,
When peace returns, to know our love will last.

Sgt. J. H. Chave

France: Vol. I, No. 28, pg. 4   *September 2, 1944*

Letter To My Girl

What can I say, dearest one, when the way
Of a dream is a detour through Hell?
What promise remains when the world is insane,
And to breath is the whim of a shell?

Clouds above move about, echoed sounds of a shout,
Free and constant, and transient too.
From these strengths above comes a strength to my love,
And my heart, and my soul are with you.

Sgt. P. Rosenbaum

Belgium: Vol. II, No. 7, pg. 4   *September 23, 1944*

The Lively Lady

A foreign Prince did once import,
A flea with sex appeal;
Her antics were a treat to watch,
Her name it was Lucille.

But she lived for love, and love alone,
Celibacy was not her state;
And soon she found that which she sought;
A true and loving mate.

Conventional things then soon occurred,
They raised a family;
Then they in turn all married,
And lived most happily.

Today you find them everywhere,
They play and jump and flirt;
I even found a loving pair,
Making whoopee in my shirt.

G. R. Simpson

Italy: Vol. III, No. 19, pg. 5   *December 16, 1944*

A Soldier's Love

I know that I shall love you
Until the day I die;
As long as there's a day and night;
As long as birds still fly.
My love will grow with every hour,
And every day and year.
And life will be a blessing, Love,
As long as you are near.

But if something should happen, Love
To keep us far apart,
You always will be near me
Forever in my heart.
And if by chance the Gods of war
Decide to seal my fate,
Somewhere in other solitudes
My heart for you will wait.

My love for you is greater
Than the stars, the sun, the moon.
And my heart is thinking of you
Every morning night and noon.
I know the love you have for me
Will always be the same.
So the waiting, be it long or short,
Will not bring too much pain.

L/Cpl. E. C. Doyle

Belgium: Vol. II, No. 149, pg. 2   March 10, 1945

Soldier's Wife

This week she lives in Surrey,
Next week she lives in Kent.
She never knows precisely where
The next month will be spent.
It's not what you'd exactly call
The stablest form of love,
But she wouldn't change for anything,
'Cause she's a soldier's wife.

A minute here, a minute there,
An hour or maybe two
Together, then he's on the move.
New orders have come through,
She has no home, no friends, no time
To linger; like a knife
The call of duty parts them,
And she's just a soldier's wife.

Poor, lonely and bewildered,
She waits for that great day
When sunshine once more bathes the world
And storm-clouds roll away.
No more will duty call him,
Gone will be the war and strife,
And no more, except in mem'ry
Will she be a soldier's wife.

S/Sgt F.J. Nethercut

W. Europe: Vol. III, No. 95, pg. 4   July 14, 1945

VII

Peace & Freedom

Canadian Battle Song

They had a vision; that's why they came.
From far-off hilltops, voices called their name;
Glory and Death vied for the hearts of men,
And they, responding, cared not which called them.

They knew the task, the quick unfettering
Of Freedom, held in bond by Slavery's king.
They knew the ransom price that must be paid
And knowing, heeded not, were not afraid.

They wanted only reck'ning, swift and sure;
To fight battles quickly, not endure
Attrition's warfare or prolonged delay.
They sailed upon a gray December day.

Full forty months they waited for their chance;
Once they embarked for Norway, twice for France;
But always adverse fortune stepped between.
Their only feats were those that "might have been".

And then there was Dieppe--but say no more;
Magnificent it was, but never war.
They bought the safety of a million men,
Returned and built their strength to fight again.

But stay, the hand that shapes affairs of men
Was rounding out the pattern even then.
Canada's die was cast at Alemein--
First gleaming link in Monty's victory chain.

For when the Eighth struck there and battled through
The vaunted German line, a rendezvous
Was written in the Book of Doom
And nurtured in the Future's secret womb.

That rendezvous was kept one summer's morn,
On Sicily's beaches, by the light of dawn.
The Red Patch and the white Crusader's Shield
Were fused in fire upon the battle field.

The red for valor stood; the white for hope,
Which followed in their wake, as from each slope
The Hun was driven and the island freed
Of tyranny and lust and German greed.

O, Canada, thy sons were battle tried
And proven! Think on this with sober pride.
They wrote their name in stars across the sky
And, while stars shine, that fame can never die.

Share, then, the vision bright that they defined;
Ensure that their high courage is enshrined
In deeds, not words. Even the dead can be
Remembered best if those who live stay free.

R. E. Beamish

Italy: Vol. I, No. 77, pg. 5   *May 6, 1944*

Ortona

A proud and pretty town it was,
Along the Adriatic coast;
A place we'll long remember and
A place of which we long will boast.

For there it was the Canadians fought
A battle long and hard,
To oust the Nazi paratroops,
Who fought us yard by yard.

Each building was a fortress and
Each street a killing ground.
We took them on as best we could
And fought them round by round.

As each blow fell, we took it well,
Fought back with all our might,
Each foot we gained, a victory for
The cause we knew was right.

And when the final bell rang out
Our counter blows were counted,
One hand was raised by One Above--
For peace--a task surmounted.

J. L. Thirlwell

Italy: Vol. I, No. 95, pg. 5   *May 27, 1944*

Remember Pontecorvo

On the road from Pontecorvo,
As you move down from the line,
There are rows of wooden crosses
All painted white, and fine.
They're the headstones for the fallen,
Who underneath do lie;
They're the men who came from Canada
To fight for Peace--and die.
They're the stalwart sons of Freedom
That came from farm and mine;
They're the stalwart sons of Canada
Who broke the Hitler Line.

As you walk through rows of crosses,
As quiet as the spring,
The wanton breezes murmur
"The Torch to you, we fling."
They've caught the Torch, and held it,
And kept it bright aflame,
And dying, throw the challenge--
"We expect of you, the same."
When history is written
And we all in Peace abide,
Remember Pontecorvo,
And the men who fought and died.

P. J. Power

Italy: Vol. II, No. 6, pg. 5   *July 8, 1944*

Lest You Forget

Come hither, thou, but softly tread
For this is sacred ground. And we
Who heard the call to help set free
The peoples of the world, lie dead
Beneath these rows of crosses white;
We rest the while, no more to fight.

When guns be still'd and tumult cease,
And wars no more disturb the world,
When Freedom's flag is full unfurl'd,
And nations live again in Peace,
Keep thou in mind the goal we set;
We shall not sleep if you forget.

For Freedom's sake did we endure
The pangs of war. We do but ask
That you will carry on our task
And everlasting Peace ensure.
Work, strive for this; goodwill maintain,
Then will our lives be not in vain.

"Mel"

Italy: Vol. II, No. 18, pg. 5   *July 22, 1944*

Cassino

The dusky hills roll back from plains,
Mysterious, silent, eerie,
Held in their rocky crags remains
The secret of the Liri.
For blood ran red and stained the snow- -
The dead lie on the plains below.

If hills but had a voice to raise,
What wondrous tales they'd tell
Of courage, daring, sacrifice,
Of men who lived in Hell.
For bloody battles raged on high
'Midst peaks beneath the Italian sky.

One spot we know will
In constant memory stay- -
Cassino, Monastery Hill,
And the price we had to pay.
But pay we did, and told a world
That Freedom's flag would stay unfurled.

To those who saw that shattered mound
Where once a town has stood,
The stench of death, the gaping ground,
The charred and splintered wood
All told a story, sad yet true,
Of what a world at war can do.

Thus, when I saw those blackened trees,
Their shattered limbs outflung
I thought, like hills, they cannot speak,
Yet witnessed feats unsung.
And many deeds of valour will
Be locked forever in "That Hill".

George Downie
Italy: Vol. II, No. 30, pg. 5   *August 5, 1944*

Request of The Fallen

We lay them down in foreign lands
Beneath the cold, damp sod;
Their work on earth accomplished,
Their souls we give to God.

Brave lads of our Dominion
From east unto the west
Begrudging not their sacrifice--
God grant their last request.

Let not future generations
As they journey on through life,
Be called upon to settle
Another world of strife.

Give nations, Lord, the power
Of vision strong, to see
That a world of friendly neighbours
A peaceful world would be.

Let men heed not to colour,
Nor criticize of creed;
Abolish, Good Lord, from them
Their greatest foe--of greed.

Then we, Thy sons, the fallen,
That freedom might remain,
Will sleep in peace well knowing,
We have not died in vain.

J. W. Oldford

Italy: Vol. II, No. 78, pg. 5   *September 30, 1944*

Why Canadians Fight

So, why are we fighting, you ask us?
Our hearts swell with pride when we say
We fight for Democracy's freedom
Our forefathers schooled us that way.
We fight for a noble Dominion;
That houses the things we adore,
We're proud it is ''Nullus Secundus,''
All we ask for is peace, nothing more.

We fight to protect all our loved ones;
All the things that they cherish so dear.
So their future might be one of gladness,
Not a life full of heartaches and fear.
We fight for the cause that is precious;
We're proud we can stand and defy
Herr Hitler, who Freedom would banish.
With God's help we'll win it or die.

CQMS B. M. Parker

Belgium: Vol. II, No. 25, pg. 4   October 14, 1944

Tribute[7]

They lie in fields,
These men
Who fought so bravely for the right;
And died so bravely that other men might live,
To love and laugh, as once they did before.
They lie in fields. Where crosses
Mark their graves
From here to France's shore.

Can we forget them?
Hardly!
Would we forget the men
Whose fingers, numb with cold
Clutch guns butts till the last,
And died
So that the old and the young
And sick and poor
Could live in peace?
They did not die in vain,
For we who knew the pain
And suffering they met
Will not forget.

J. A. Aisliett

Belgium: Vol. II, No. 73, pg. 4   *December 9, 1944*

Democracy's Flag

Our flag unfurled, will fly above
A symbol of the life we loved;
A flag which means to you and me
Freedom in democracy.

While over there across the Rhine
We know that things are not so fine.
They have no say, those folks across;
They have dictators for a boss.
They dare not think the way they like;
They dare not cease their losing fight.

But we're proud to be, yes, you and me,
Members of democracy.
We're proud and glad to raise our eyes
To where the Union Jack still flies.

L/Cpl. E. C. Doyle

Belgium: Vol. III, No. 6, pg. 2   *March 31, 1945*

Ode to Canada's Fighting Indians

A man lies still in the starlit night.
A shell lands close, perhaps there are more.
What is this thing for which men fight?
The freedom of our land, forever more.

The man looks up, we see his face.
His face is dark. His eyes how they shine!
His hair is black. What is his race?
His mud-caked features are rugged and fine.

Let's follow his thoughts, to see who he is,
For surely we've seen him some other place.
He gazes round, the night is his
His thoughts wonder, we'll soon know his race.

He thinks of some far off beaten trail
Where the deer and moose have passed.
He thinks of the beaver and the quail,
And the many moons since he saw them last.

He thinks of the bear, the shaggy beast;
Of the running stream, and silvery trout
From which he has made many a feast
Or the porcupine, the lazy lout.

What brought him here to this far off land,
Where death is ever constant and near,
Where no more he hears the waves on the sand,
Of some small lake which to him was dear?

The Great White Father called his sons,
Into the battle for the right to be free.
He answered the call, he is proud to be one,
And now he is proud to die for his country.

140

Hark! That whisper which startles the night.
Some instinct warns, 'tis the enemy.
His thoughts are gone, he must fight
For Canada the home of the brave and free.

Gnr. B. R. Nadjiwan

W. Europe: Vol. III, No. 47, pg. 4   May 19, 1945

May Fight, 1945

At last an hour of mighty triumph strikes,
The Teuton beast has fallen to his knees,
After our years against perverted power- -
For providential Justice thus decrees.

Millions are now rejoicing in this hour,
Freed from the bondage of an evil brain,
Freed at the cost of countless brave young lives
And broken minds and bodies wracked with pain.

But in this hour of triumph we must not
Forget the barbarous Oriental yet;
Or Singapore, Hong Kong, the Phillipines,
Pearl Harbour and the others in his net.

The time has not arrived when we may rest,
And laugh and say ''The dirty job is done.''
Complacence now is criminal at best,
To those who still are fighting bravely on.

So let us keep our heads and use our hands
And work to make this place a better world
Until our task is fully and well done
And peace may raise her banner full unfurled.

Lt. Stanley S. W. Cole

W. Europe: Vol. III, No. 53, pg. 4   May 26, 1945

Visions of Waterloo

I have seen the ruin of cities,
I have glimpsed a nation's woe,
I have viewed the grim destruction
In the wake of a ruthless foe.

But emotion surged within me,
Linking ancient with the new:
As I gazed in awe-struck wonder
O'er the fields of Waterloo.

Gone the deadly sunken roadway
Where an army plunged to doom.
Gone the trees within whose shadows,
"Conquered conqueror" wept in gloom.

Not a vestige of the conflict
That destroyed a tyrant's thrall,
Save the panorama pictured
On the famed museum wall.

But the stately spires of Brussels
Proudly glint the fading day
Where the warriors stepped to music
Ere they sallied to the fray.

North and east a battle rages,
And a tryrant quakes once more;
As he feels the force of justice
Pressing on to close the score.

Through the ages Sons of England,
Bring relief to tortured lands.
And flags of liberation
Wave in Anglo-Saxon hands.

In the flames of retribution
Chains of bondage melt away;
Nippon, Fascist, Luftwaffe, Wehrmacht,
Hohenzollen, Grande Armée.

J. H. Townsend

W. Europe: Vol. III, No. 53, pg. 4   May 26, 1945

Peace and Spring

Silent now the cannon's roar,
No whine of bullets overhead,
As though the very things that killed
Are now, themselves, all dead.

Nature, as though to ease her wounds,
And hide the war's drear mess,
Has blossomed forth in many ways
With spring's bright loveliness.

Shell holes edged in green grass lace
Look less like cankerous sores.
A rubbled house without a roof
Has ivy 'round its doors.

Children play and pick the flowers
Within the fringe of wood,
Where, seemingly, just yesterday,
A row of cannons stood.

Fields that but a while ago
Held many a gory scene,
Now echo to death's cry no more
For they are lush and green.

Every bush and every tree
Echo God's great will
As once again He seems to say
"Peace on earth, to all good will."

Sgt. R. W. Evans

W. Europe: Vol. III, No. 65, pg. 4   June 9, 1945

Holland, May, 1945

I passed a windmill swinging in the sun--
Great sails that creaking turned; and I did stand
Unwatched by sheep that gazed on either hand,
And thought of those whose lives had new begun.
Nor could I hope to fully understand
What "freedom" means to boys, with voices shrill,
Who were dancing there beside the mill,
Who knew that fear had vanished from their land.
My mind went back to safe years in the past--
In priceless freedom spent I cared not how,
Indifferent as the sheep beside me now
Had I then been to liberty. At last
I shared their joy of life reborn in Spring;
As I walked on my soul began to sing.

Cpl. Don Nelson

W. Europe: Vol. III, No. 65, pg. 4   June 9, 1945

Let Us Not Fail

Let us not fail our fallen dead
Who died for you and me
We must not fail our fallen men
Who died to keep us free.

Let us not fail all those who lie
Beneath the cold, damp sod.
They died because they knew no fear
But had their faith in God.

Let us not fail our comrades dead.
They did their very best.
It's up to us to see that they Have their eternal rest.

Let us not fail as we did before,
To end all wars and strife.
We have a torch to hold on high
From those who gave their life.

Let us not fail to pray to God
That they who sleep beneath the sod
Will never have to think that we
Have failed to keep the whole world free.

L/Cpl. G. W. Moor

W. Europe: Vol. III, No. 77, pg. 4   June 23, 1945

Sonnet

The storm of war in Europe now is spent;
The world, its eyes re-opened, looks around
And sees four countries' rubble on the ground,
Beneath whose dust lies dust of those who went
Away so gaily, though their families lent
For once and all. Have they the reason found
For losing men whose lives with peace abound?
Dare they, the lonely, wonder what is meant?

But soon this thought a ray of comfort brings
As surely, swiftly comes to us a light
When once again the song of freedom rings.
Above, the skylark sings by day; and night
Is now a time for rest. It was these things
For which they fought their truly glorious fight.

Gnr. D. L. Sinclair

W. Europe: Vol. III, No. 83, pg. 5   June 30, 1945

The Great Battle

If you are one of the high score men
And you get repatriated;
And you land in civvie street again,
Supposedly elated - -

If you stay where you do not fraternize,
And occupation bores;
And visions are always before your eyes
Of fair Canadian shores - -

If you hail for far-off Burma
O'er the vast Pacific foam;
Where entrenched in terra firma
You will surely pine for home - -

There is always one great battle
Resplendent now with strife;
The last and final battle - -
The endless one for life.

Pte. M. Holmes

W. Europe: Vol. III, No. 83, pg. 5   June 30, 1945

Live On - But Don't Forget

In the shadow of the cross,
before the setting sun,
Lies an ever silent heart,
whose life had just begun.
No more it beats with happiness
when joys of life are met.
Now it is still, for you and I--
live on, but don't forget.

Just a soldier in his 'teens who
had left a life to give,
Yet brave enough to let it die,
to let our freedom live!
And when his blood was flowing fast
he held no sad regret.
He paid the price our freedom asked--
live on, but don't forget!

Somewhere a mother mourns for him,
within a saddened home.
Her boy now lies beneath a cross
so far across the foam.
Because of their great sacrifice
a sun of peace can set,
So, for the ones that set for us,
live on--but don't forget.

Gnr. H. A. Russell

W. Europe: Vol. III, No. 119, pg. 4   August 11, 1945

For Those Who Come

The clarion call, "Arise, to Arms,"
Rang forth upon a peaceful world.
We sallied forth in quick reply
Our mould'ring battle flags unfurled.

We sallied forth upon a world
Imperiled by fearful fate
Of harsh and cruel tyranny
Beneath the lashing whip hate.

Oppression hovered o'er the world,
Its evil talons reached to clasp
And crush the soul and mind of man,
Within its foul and clutching grasp.

The evil hosts of lust and greed,
With unjust power's willing nod,
Laid waste the hopes and dreams of men,
Left want and sorrow where they trod.

We fought and strove through times so dark.
The mind could scarcely see the light
Of cherished victory shining through
The battle's dark and stormy night.

We fought with heart and soul until
Our righteous cause gained victory just,
And hatred, greed and cruelty lay
Destroyed and bleeding in the dust.

We fought, we gave our lives, our dreams,
As once our fathers did in yore.
We fought that those who came behind
Should never know the curse of war.

We fought for you, and for this world,
And for our way of life and thought,
Will you, the ones who come behind
Preserve the things for which we fought?

E. Z. Anderson

W. Europe: Vol. III, No. 130, pg. 4   August 25, 1945

The Peace

The shouting and the tumult dies
As noise of battle and deathly cries
Fade into the darkening past.
The glorious day has come at last.

We who have come from distant lands
Have carried the torch in our own free hands,
And now that victory is here,
Let's win the peace, throughout the year.

Sgt. Ben Pelchovitz

W. Europe: Vol. IV, No. 9, pg. 4   September 15, 1945

To Our Emblem

If I must grow old with vanity,
Let it be pride in my own country.
Let me gaze at the leaf growing strong and free
Up at the top of a maple tree.
Let me think of our emblem and for what it stands:
For this our home our native land.
It stands for the youth who at country's call
Answered the bugle, then gave their all
Not for themselves or for vain glory
But for unborn children, and you and me:
For freedom from want, freedom from fear,
Freedom of conscience, unchallenged, clear.
That we worship our Maker, abide His plan,
Free from the scorn of any man.
To uplift the downtrodden, defend the poor,
And to teach the children that they endure.
Not alone for themselves, but for liberty,
For justice and right, and for equality.
To assuage the anguish of those in need
Regardless of colour, race and creed:
To stand by our country through sun or rain,
To glory in all that's Canadian:
To remember the tears of our mothers whose sons
Died in the blast, facing enemy guns:
For the Canadians dead in Picardy,
And for those who sleep in Normandy:
For our heroes who fought at the Falaise mound:
For the sanctity of Vimy ground:
For all that is noble, strong and true,
To the Maple Leaf a salute to you.
If I grow old with vanity,
Let it be pride in my own country.
Let me gaze at the leaf growing strong and free,
Up at the top of a maple tree.
Let me think of our emblem and for what it stands,
In this, our own, our native land.

Edward, B. Folger
W. Europe: Vol. IV, No. 27, pg. 5   October 6, 1945

VIII

Afterwards…

These Things Remain

The meadows lush with Spring time,
And birdsong sounding gay,
The golden tints of Autumn,
Trees in their green array.

The song of running water,
Fresh green of springing grain,
The gleam of new-turned furrows
Sweet-smelling, after rain.

Cows grazing in a pasture,
Trails through a winter wood,
The busy stir of harvest,
We know that these are good.

These things shall last the lifetime
Of this old, battered earth.
After the war's mad frenzy
These are the things of worth.

E. Dowson

Italy: Vol. I, No. 119, pg. 5   *June 24, 1944*

About The P.O.W.'S

I wonder what they think and dream
inside that Compound wire,
For they are human with their love,
And hate, and heart's desire.

These men have steered a lurching tank;
Dropped bombs on London town,
And from the lurking submarine
Have sent our convoys down.

Wearing that alien uniform
That we were taught to dread,
They do not look so fearsome now,
And somehow hate lies dead.

I understand that far-off look--
I know their anxious yearning;
My loved ones, too, are far away
And my heart, too, is burning.

But as I sit and ponder
Upon their dastard feats,
Pity dies within me,
And red-hot anger beats.

They bombed our open cities--
(My kindred lived in one),
And shot at helpless refugees
Where war-torn roadways run.

They sank the lone tramp steamer,
And as she settled down,
Turned loose their fire on open boats
To watch our seamen drown.

So as I watch the prisoners
Inside the Compound gate,
And know their deeds to me and mine- -
Have I not cause to hate?

E. A. Dowson

Italy: Vol. I, No. 125, pg. 5   *July 1, 1944*

Soliloquy

I wander the hills without a care,
With no thought of the dark to come.
The church bells ring the evening prayer;
The day, its hours have spun.
The scene is one of peace and calm
Where once the battle raged.
A soothing, quiet, restful balm
The wounds of war have laved.

It brings to mind the fallen dead,
Those whose thirst of war did sate
Who know the taste of daily bread:
Love, toil, tears and hate.
"Oh will the lesson be never learned,"
The voice of our dead still cry,
"Again we throw the torch, once spurned,
If the light goes out- - -In vain we die."

The night is here and darks the day,
Now each footstep I must grope.
He sends a moon to guide the way,
Oh send our souls some hope!
How do we walk in this darkened Love
If even our dead know fright?
Oh mighty God of Peace and Power,
Keep the Torch of Justice alight.

P. Marks

Italy: Vol. II, No. 12, pg. 5   *July 15, 1944*

When You Return

(sent by F. E. Bender, CPC)

When you return I shall not question you
On all your little deeds since that far day
Time wedged our paths apart. I shall not say
As others might, who missed your presence, too:
"How did you like the town of so and so?"
Or some such phrase friends utter, unconcerned;
What use are casual words to those who learned
One day, in silence, all they need to know?
I shall abide my time and, when, at last
The clamour and the greeting all are done,
Our eyes shall meet, and silently, as one,
We shall relive one moment in the past,
And you shall know, though lips let no words fall,
That in my heart you did not leave at all.

Anonymous

Italy: Vol. II, No. 102, pg. 5   *October 28, 1944*

History's Roundabout

In Flander's Fields through mud and snow,
We place new crosses between the rows
That mark the place our fathers fell,
Who died to save us from this hell.
But now we lie here, young and old,
Beneath the poppies, wet and cold,
To make for you a living place,
Free from fear to come and go
In Flander's Fields.

We caught the torch our fathers threw,
And now we pass it on to you.
We hope you've learned another bit
Because we failed to keep it lit.
And now our fathers we shall meet,
To join them in peaceful sleep,
While trodden down with weary feet,
The poppies grow in Flander's Field.

Sgt. R. McBride

Italy: Vol. III, No. 36, pg. 4   *January 6, 1945*

The Last Break Off

When they give you the last break off,
And you turn on your heel to go
Out the big iron gates past the sentry,
To the others who love you so,
Will you think of the boys who won't be there,
Who still sleep 'neath the distand sod?
Will you think of the ones who sent you back,
Will you offer you thanks to God?

Will you offer a word of sympathy
To a mother who's lost her son,
Or a wife who has lost her husband
In the battle against the Hun?
Or will you pass on with never a word,
Or with maybe a wave of your hand
To the gray-haired old lady who stands alone
Watching the troops disband?

Yes, boys, when the battle is over,
And we're back in our homes again,
We mustn't forget there'll be many
Whose hearts will be heavy with pain.
And a clasp of the hand will lighten the load,
Or a word make it easier to bear
The fact that a loved one is calling
That he gave all he had over there.

So let's not forget in our happiness
That our duty is only half done.
We will have to tell of the brave exploits
That have been done by some husband or son.
Let's not try to take all the glory,
But acknowledge and reverently lend.
The times we won through victory
Was by simply trusting in God.

Submitted by Pte. B. S. Barry, Author unknown
Italy: Vol. III, No. 72, pg. 4   February 17, 1945

Hommage et Anniversaire

L'année a fui, le froid revient,
Les soirs sont solitaires.
On trinque, on fume, on se souvient
Des morts, des braves, des téméraires.

Ils étaient peu. Il y a un an
A Bernardi, ce lieu fameux,
Où, de leurs forces, baignés de sang,
Ils tenaient fermé, ces vrais Vingt-Deux.

Hommages à vous, héros dormants,
Témoins muets du prix payé.
Hommanges à vous qui étes vivants,
Soldats, sergeant, et officier.

Hommage à vous du "petit fracas",
Petits de nom, grands de succès,
Qui teniez ferme a la Casa.
Laissant la gloire aux écossais.

Ainsi pensif, ce soir je bois
Silencieusement mon vin,
A ceux reposant sous leur croix
Et je murmure, "Je me souviens."

Sgt. G. A. P.

Italy: Vol. III, No. 96, pg. 4   *March 17, 1945*

163

Anniversary Tribute

The year has flown by and returned the cold weather;
Our evenings are lonely, joyless.
We drink, smoke and remember
The dead, brave, fearless.

Just a year ago, few in number
At Bernardi, that place now renowned,
Wounded, bleeding, they did not surrender,
Those true Vingt-Deux, they held their ground.

We salute you, heroes now sleeping,
Silent witnesses of the price you paid.
We salute you, those who are living,
Soldiers, sergeants, officers... saved.

We salute you, the single-hearted,
Nameless, but now men of renown,
Who at the casa never yielded,
Leaving the Scots to hold the crown.

So tonight, deep in thought, drinking
My wine silently,
To those under their crosses lying,
"I remember", I murmur sadly.

Translated by
Jane Morgan

Point and Disappoint

While we chased the Hun in Italy,
And thirsted for his blood;
While we slept in leaky pup-tents,
Or slithered through the mud;
While we saw the lights of Pompeii
Or the snappy babes of Rome,
We none the less looked forward to
The end of war... and home.

We yearned for good old Canada,
And its not so lovely clime.
We hoped we might arrive there
In the good old summer time.
But though the show has ended,
And it is getting well in June,
It's anything but certain
That we'll be leaving soon.

Though the folks back there are practicing
The ''welcome home'' refrain,
And their letters say ''Just wire us,
We'll meet you at the train.''
Though the high-point boys are eager
To see all their folks so dear,
They're beginning to have suspicions
That it will not be this year.

It plainly has us puzzled,
There is not the slightest doubt.
We figure one point system,
Then there's one more to dope out.
And we've used up many pencils
'Til it nearly has us broke.
But to four or five year Joes,
Well, pal, it's not a joke.

Though we like it here in Holland,
And the Dutch are friendly blokes,
We've been away for four long years
And we'd like to see our folks.
Though with the ''doper-outers''
We have no quarrel to pick.
But please think up one point system
That is fairly sure to stick.

Tom McMahon

W. Europe: Vol. III, No. 77, pg. 4   June 23, 1945

After Rehab

Yes, I can see them now in years to be,
Down in the basement of the Legion Hall,
Recalling through the haze of alcohol,
Days prior to, and following VE.
I wonder, when we're talking, you and me,
Letting our fancy chose what to recall,
If we'll begin to think, "Why damn it all,
Those were the days. Boy, bring another three."

Thus school days are the best years of your life--
After they are gone. And the farthest fields
are green--
Before the mist of time has slipped betwen
My eyes and these receding days of strife.
Let me write here and underline it well--
Old Sherman had it right, pal, WAR IS HELL.

Pte. J. M. Stedmond

W. Europe: Vol. III, No. 89, pg. 3   July 7, 1945

The German Scene

I sat beneath a friendly fir
And gazed upon a tranquil scene
Of red-topped houses snuggling in
A paradise of nature's green.
A slow and quiet flowing stream
Meandered through the valley lush;
The balmy air seemed laden with
A breathless, quiet, peaceful hush.

How false this scene of gentle peace!
Misleading to the heart and eye.
These quiet woods and shady lanes
Have echoed to the War Lord's cry.
The roll of drum, the flash of steel,
The crashing cannon's angry roar,
Here flourished in the fiendish glare
Of Nazi hate and lust for war.

And though the War Lord cries no more,
The cannon and the drum now rest,
Within the quiet valley's homes
Hate burns within the human breast.
I lingered 'neath the friendly fir
And pondered o'er the ways of men,
And wondered how this eauty spot
Could be an evil Nazi den.

Zeke

W. Europe: Vol. III, No. 113, pg. 4   August 4, 1945

German Soil

No banners, no waving cheers,
No smiling, tearfull eyes
Meet ours as noonday nears,
Moving sleepily through the skies.
But a few were present then,
A man, a woman, a child,
Silent, staring, wondering when
Or where, and yet reconciled
That they yet lived; a mortal three
In a body, a soul, and free!

From one field to another's part
We had moved; but the same
Yet two wide worlds apart.
One a pulsating heart, the other pain
Struck hard and low; a wedge
Burning through and bleeding deep
Beyond the body's lifeless edge.
And now in this defeat they weep
Moistening the soil's eager brow
Where a seed just sown may grow.

Richard O'Brien

W. Europe: Vol. III, No. 130, pg. 4   August 25, 1945

Time Marches On

Time marches on and the guns are still,
While over on a distant hill
A farmer pauses 'neath the sun
And thinks of battles long since won.

His plough has hit a heavy stone
And as the bird songs brightly drone,
He stoops to see what he has found
Beneath the wet and clay-like ground.

It is a rifle, rusted now,
Turned up again beneath the plough,
A German weapon, meant to kill,
But now so useless on the hill.

He smiles at relics of a day
When battle noise was heard that way.
Time marches on, the guns are still,
He turns again towards the hill.

Pte. Roy Williams

W. Europe: Vol. IV, No. 9, pg. 4   September 15, 1945

A Soldier's Thoughts

I stand upon this foreign strand:
Behind me lies a war-torn land.
Before me stretches restless sea,
No ship in sight to carry me
Back to my home, my native heath,
With tranquil skies to live beneath.

My thoughts return to years just gone.
Thank God war's hell has passed beyond
Wherein were days when not we knew...
If morrow's sunrise we should view:
The tearing steel our bodies felt,
We've by a fallen comrade knelt:
Should he be sleeping, ne'er to wake,
God ease the heart his death may break.

And those of us with yet long life,
May we prevent all future strife,
With all its sorrow, pain and tears.
Let peaceful be the coming years.
Let us in memory ever keep
Sacred thought for those who sleep
In silent graves in foreign sand.
They've sacrificed their all for man.

But life must always forward go.
For us who wait here time is slow.
We long for home, we curse, we pray.
Do we move faster? Not a day.
Impatient then, we build at best
Within our minds, our future quest.
A plan of things we'll build some day
When at long last we're home to stay.

There's none so great as native soil,
Whereon to rest, to play or toil.
Our Canada we'll build with pride
May God our destiny so guide,
That sons of yours will ever fight
For honesty, for truth and right.

J. H. Young

W. Europe: Vol. IV , No. 15, pg. 4   September 22, 1945

Aftermath

In a little Belgian frontier town,
'Twixt rubble and decay,
A peaceful, tiny, cemet'ry
In slumbering beauty lay.

Upon a bench which time had worn,
And nails had lost their grasp,
I saw a man with head bowed low,
And heart and hands in clasp.

For him no happy victory,
Though battle cry was o'er:
No kindly friends who could replace
What he had lost by war.

Both wife and son, through death are gone,
His home chaotic ruin,
And he too old to pick up life
From which has gone the bloom.

Yes, there he sits in his despair,
O'er burdened with such grief,
That only death can set him free
And bring him life's release.

So, though I know in years to come
Peace on earth will reign:
The memory of his worn-torn soul,
Forever will remain.

Kjaer Jensen

W. Europe: Vol. IV. No. 44, pg. 5   October 27, 1945

173

Notes

1   Taken from a small volume of verses entitled ''Scattered Leaves'', which was composed earlier in England. It was published under the auspices of the British Author's Press.

2   F/O Davey was killed in action. The poem was found among his papers.

3   From a collection entitled ''Booklet of Poems'' (Rome, February, 1945) by the Public Relations Services. Major Alex R. Campbell was killed in action. This poem was found on his body.

4   Major Paul Triquet was awarded the V. C. His portrait is in the War Museum, Ottawa.

5   From ''Booklet of Poems (see note 3). This poem was contributed by a British poet who was associated with the Canadian Forces in Italy.

6   Written by an unknown Canuck while in action at Rimini.

7   A tribute to the men of the Third Division.

8   Third Prize winner in the First Canadian Army Troops competition.

9   Written after the Battle of the Scheldt, Holland in October 1944. Robert Gray was later wounded and evacuated to England. The poem appears in an article, ''The Leopold Ordeal'', of the Legion Magazine (Vol. 62, No. 4) of October, 1987.

10   The SSR referred to in the last line is the South Saskatchewan Regiment.

11   "Bing" refers to "Bing Coughlin," cartoonist for the Maple Leaf.

Index of Poets

Heath, Craig

Higgs, H/Capt.
Stanley E.

Holliday, D. B.

Holmes, Pte. M.

"J" (Italy, '44)

Jeffery, Bdr. E. G.

Jensen, Kjaer

E. K.

Kelly, Drv. Joseph

Keyte, Cpl. L.

King, Charles

Larke, A. E.

Liverpool, Cpl.
J. A.

F. W. M.

McBride, Sgt. R.

MacDonald, Pte.
S. R.

MacDougall, Sgt.
C. W.

McGinnis, A. P.

McMahon, Tom

Maidens, Cpl. B. C.

Marks, P.

Meade, Sgt. D.

"Mel"
Mont, Pte. J. M.

Moor, L/Cpl. G. W.

Munro, Pte. M. D.

Mycock, Pte.

Nadjiwan, Gnr. B. R.

Nelson, Cpl. Don

Nethercut, S/Sgt.
F. J.

Nickerson, Margaret

O'Brien, Richard

Oldford, J. W.

Ord, W/C J. D.

G. A. P., Sgt.

J. M. P.

Parish, James

Parker, CQMS B. M.

Parkes, Pte. H. E.

Parr, Gnr, Bill

Patterson, L/Cpl.
G. G.

Pearson, James

Pelchovitz, Sgt.
Ben

Poulton, R.

Powell, G. W.

Power, P. J.
"Ray"

Rogers, John A.

Rose, G. A.

Rosenbaum, Sgt. P.

Ross, Sgt. G. R. H.

Russel, Gnr. H. A.

Semezuk, Jack

Shiels, L/Cpl.
G. S.

Simpson, G. R.

Sinclair, Gnr.
D. L.

Smith, Sgt. D. H.

Smith, Pte. Jack

Stedmond, Pte.
J. M.

Steel, Sgt. A.

Sterling, M. St. C.

Thirlwell, J. L.

Thompson, T. H.

Tompkins, Pte. T.

Townsend, J. H.

J. R. W.

Warren, Sgmn. Don

Welch, Pte. John H.

Wheelock, Cpl.
(forwarded by)

Wherry, Matthew

Whittaker, Sgmn.
R. H.

Williams, Pte. Roy

Wilson, Trp. L. T.

Young, J. H.

Zeke

Note: G.W. Powell also wrote
under the pseudonyms Sgt. E.
K. and McGinnis, A.P.

List of Poems